Easy Peasy Crop

A Comprehensive Guide to Container Gardening for the Modern City Dweller, the Practical Solution to Growing Your Own Fruits, Vegetables and Herbs in Tiny Urban Spaces

Landan B.

GIFT FOR YOU

Thank you for purchasing this book! To show our appreciation, we thought we'd send you a bonus in the form of a **FREE mini E-book**!

We think you'll enjoy **SELF-SUFFICIENT GARDENING, 10 Essential Crops for the Practical Gardener**.

On top of receiving this PDF download, you'll receive updates on new publications and free offerings!

Scan the code below to sign up at our newsletter and claim your gift:

http://bit.ly/3fhPT4q

Table of Contents

Introduction

Gardening has been reinvented. There are no more excuses for not planting a seed and growing your food. If properly conducted, you can grow your own food anywhere, all while bringing a beautiful passion and aesthetic to your home. Small spaces? No yard? No time? No problem. You can do it with container gardening. Container gardening allows you to grow your food, medicine, and ornamental plants in a more efficient way than traditional gardening. You can grow more food, in less space, with less time and energy. It's an excellent tool for the modern resident who wants to go back to their agrarian roots without having to reshape your life in the countryside. It's also an excellent tool for those with gardening space who want to maximize their space and time. If properly executed, you can eat from your container garden even within the confines of a small urban apartment or home. Aside from the delicious food, container gardening also beautifies your home while building a hobby and passion that will bring meaning and joy to your life.

Container gardening is as the name implies. Growing plants in above-ground containers. This allows you to grow plants anywhere, even above paved and impermeable surfaces. You can find containers of any size to match the fit and style of your home. Container gardening allows you to have more control of your plants by giving you jurisdiction of the soil, water, light, and perfect location for the plants of your choice. Having the ability to move your containers can even allow you to extend your season by moving your containers into strategic locations. If properly executed container gardening can be much easier and time-efficient than traditional gardening. It removes the need for shoveling, tilling, weeding, and all the muddiness involved with a common garden. Meanwhile, it gives your home a novel green and living aesthetic that cannot be achieved in any other way.

An ancient Chinese proverb says "The best time to plant a tree was twenty years ago. The second-best time is now." The same goes for container gardening. The fact you picked up this book suggests you are probably familiar with all the uncertainties that exist in our modern world. Uncertainties about what's in your food and what the long-term health consequences are. Uncertainties about conventional medicines and the pharmaceutical doctors readily prescribe. Uncertainties about your environmental and ethical impacts and what it means to our planet and disadvantaged communities which are often exposed to harmful chemicals and low wages for its production. Uncertainties about climate change and an unstable economy that threaten modern-day agriculture and overall food security. It's possible to feel incapable of contributing anything positive to this upside-down world but know there are many channels for you to help. For me, gardening has opened these doors. Growing your food and building a relationship with what you put in your body is perhaps the best place to start turning your consumptive lifestyle around.

If you're inexperienced with gardening and feel limited by space, look no further. In this book, we will cover everything you need to know to have the most efficient and easiest to achieve garden using proven techniques for container gardening. Follow these simple strategies and philosophies and you, too, can begin being part of the forward movement!

Chapter 1: What You'll Need

Like starting any project, having everything you need is important to successfully achieve your final goal. With container gardening, you can find all you require at local stores and perhaps even lying around your home. You can start at any scale and at whatever magnitude meets your budget. In this chapter, we will cover everything you need to know for selecting the materials that best suit your needs, lifestyle, and dreams for your container garden. While there are many intricacies when it comes to choosing the right materials, they are very basic and can range in price for budget gardeners or for individuals with a bit more cash to spend.

Selecting the Right Home for Your Plants

Before all else, perhaps the best place to start is by selecting the right containers to meet your needs. In the present day, there are many different types of containers each with different characteristics that will affect your choice when selecting the perfect container. Not only are there many different sizes to choose from but different materials and attributes that will determine what is best for you. Finally, you might also want something that fits the aesthetic style of your home and the final "look" you are seeking to achieve.

Size

Size is important to consider not only because certain plants require a certain quantity of root space, but also because you need a container that fits well in your space. You will want a container not too big where it will become cumbersome and inconvenient within your space but also not too small to where you are reducing your space efficiency. For basic comfort levels, it's recommended to leave four feet of path space in your garden. This is enough for two people to comfortably walk adjacent to one another. This is particularly important in heavily trafficked areas but flexible for less used areas.

Consider this rule when choosing the right container for a particular area.

The width and the height of your pot are important to consider because they not only affect space efficiency but also will impact the types of plants you can grow and how vigorous they become. For maximizing food production and energy, wide and deep containers are most recommended. Containers 14 inches and greater in width not only allow you to grow larger plants like tomatoes and squash but allow you to mix and match different plants into a single pot! It is less labor-intensive than having to fill, water, and manage many small pots and typically will maximize the volume of soil within a specific location. Also, it is typically more economically accessible than buying many small pots for a certain area. Small containers are beneficial for fitting into tight spaces or filling in edges and space. They can also have a nice aesthetic quality when designed appropriately. As far as height is concerned, consider that taller plants need taller pots. Twenty inches is about as tall as you will ever need. At around this height, oxygen will no longer penetrate deeper into the soil creating anaerobic (low oxygen) zones that can be detrimental to your plant's health.

Types of Materials

There are many different materials to choose from when selecting your containers. What you will be most interested in comparing is the durability, cost, aesthetic, and convenience of the material. It is also important to ensure that your container does not contain any toxic materials that will contaminate your plants unless they are used solely for ornamentals.

Clay or Terracotta

These pots are some of the most common and widely available pots. They are typically an orange-earthen color and taper in diameter toward the bottom. They are aesthetically pleasing for most gardens and are made from all-natural materials. Their porous nature also helps contribute toward a more breathable pot that maintains a cooler temperature through evaporative cooling. On the downside, this evaporative behavior leads it to drying out quicker than an impermeable material. Humidity in the pores also can crack the material in freezing temperatures. These pots can also be quite fragile, diminishing their durability.

Ceramic Pots

While more expensive than other options, these are often some of the most visually pleasing pots. They are made of clay that is coated with an impermeable glaze (and often colorful designs) that gives it a shiny appearance. Some are resistant to freezing temperatures allowing you to use it all year in cold climates. Many of these pots do not have drainage holes, so check before you buy!

Fiberglass and Resin

Both are synthetic materials that are lightweight and long-lasting. They often are made to look like real terra-cotta pots.

Plastic

Plastics are durable, lightweight, cheap, and can be found just about anywhere. Finding containers made of recycled plastics can be a more sustainable option than buying new plastic. Be cautious of plastic, not all plastics are created equally! Recycling numbers on the container can help you make more informed decisions. In the United States avoid plastics labeled 3, 6, and 7.

Five-gallon buckets make for good container materials due to their abundance and relatively large size. Look for food-grade buckets and avoid any that were used for carrying harmful chemicals or paints. Another thing to consider is that plastic can quickly deteriorate when exposed to UV contained in sunlight. Thin disposable plastics are more prone to this and are not recommended. Consider keeping these pots in the shade.

Wood

Look for untreated wood. If you don't know the history of your wood, then you may be gambling with your health. Avoid old building materials that may have paint (lead was widely used in paints not too long ago), asbestos, or may have been treated with any harmful chemicals. A beautiful way to make a wooden pot is by making a "burn bowl." You can make this by burning a cavity into a piece of wood using flaming coals. You can also construct your wood containers with lumber. Properly made from the right type of wood, a wooden container can last for several years. Redwood, cedar, and teak are most recommended. Staples, nails, or screws should all be stainless steel in order to avoid rusting.

Metal

Metals can be tricky and not all will work. Galvanized steel is likely the longest lasting and trustworthy metal. Other metals are prone to rust, will not be durable, and will leave you with a dangerous unstable and rusty container. While using large old cans sounds great from the point of upcycling, beware that many cans still contain a BPA lining that may leech into your soil. Aluminum can work, but you also risk it leaching into your soil, particularly under acidic conditions.

Fabric Bags

Grow bags made from special fabrics are a good economic way of creating a large growing space with little effort. They tend to have increased evaporation and only last 7-8 seasons. Another alternative that you may have readily available are burlap bags. Consider asking a local coffee shop if they have any extra burlap sacks.

Materials to avoid: most plastic, wooden pallets, non-food grade buckets, paints (especially if you suspect it's lead-based), old building materials (may have asbestos), chemical containers, and anything with an unknown history or you may suspect is contaminated.

Drainage and Saucers

When you water your plants, water will travel downwards by the pull of gravity through the empty spaces or pores in your soil. Along its way, the water will absorb into your soil and eventually reach the bottom of your container. To prevent the stagnation of water that deteriorates the health of your soil, it is important to have drainage holes which will expel excess water. Oftentimes you may encounter containers that do not have drainage holes. While it is possible to use these pots, it is not recommended because it's likely they will hold stagnant water and lead to disease. The lack of drainage holes also reduces your container's ability to breathe and absorb oxygen. It is also not uncommon to find pots with insufficient drainage capabilities that can cause issues. The ideal size hole for drainage is about 3/4" because this provides adequate drainage while not being too big and allowing sediments to leech. For larger pots, I recommend looking for at least three drainage holes for large containers having holes 6" apart. If you are making your drainage holes make sure you know what you're doing to not damage your container. This is not recommended on concrete or glazed ceramic pots.

In some cases, you may choose to place a saucer, or drainage plate, that captures this water and prevents it from leaking onto the surface they are placed in. These saucers can keep these surfaces clean while also helping enhance your water efficiency. Water that reaches the bottom of the saucer can then be reabsorbed and pulled up through a natural wicking mechanism. This is particularly useful if your soil dries out because dry soil tends to become hydrophobic meaning it will not absorb water as it travels through your soil. Unfortunately, saucers do have their downsides. If water stays in your saucers for an extended period, it can lead to stagnation which is detrimental to the health of your soil. This can lead to root borne diseases, most notably root rot. This stagnant water can also become a breeding ground for mosquitoes. These issues are particularly prevalent in rainy climates where it's likely you may already have an abundance of water. These saucers are also typically sold separately and may add an extra cost to your shopping. With proper watering practice (explained later in the book) you will not have issues with excess water spilling nor hydrophobic soils making saucers less necessary. Where they are most recommended is in hot arid climates and for indoor gardening.

The Benefits and Downsides of Saucers	
Pros	**Cons**
-Good in arid environments	-Excess water will stagnate
-Natural wicking allows soil to absorb water from below	-Can create a breeding ground for mosquitoes
-Excess water will evaporate quickly	-Creates anaerobic conditions in soil, detrimental to soil health
-Aids water absorption in dry hydrophobic soil	-Holds too much water in rainy conditions
-Less water wasted	-Adds an extra cost
-Keeps ground surface clean	-Difficult to empty with large containers
-reduces leeching of nutrients	-Not necessary with proper watering practice
	-Could lead to salinization
	-Over watering will still overflow saucers

Choosing Your Soil

One of the many benefits of container gardening is that you have absolute control over making the right soil mix for your plants. You can easily influence your mix to meet certain criteria important to your context. Certain soils will retain more water, which is crucial in arid climates. In contrast, you may choose to have well-draining pots to increase oxygen access to your plant and reduce the risk of overwatering. Other soils may hold more nutrients allowing you to grow more vigorous heavy feeding plants.

It's important to note that the soil you should have in your containers is very different from the sediment-rich soils you'd find naturally in the ground. While you technically can use yard soil in your pots there are many different downsides to this approach. Sediment rich soils are heavy and can quickly degrade your containers. You may have an unfavorable composition like a clay-rich soil that has little air space, slow drainage, and doesn't provide adequate conditions for maximum plant growth. Ultimately you may be uncertain of the quality and safety of these soils.

For this reason, it's suggested to use an "organic" soil mix. Organic when used in this context or in "organic matter" refers to the idea that organic molecules are carbon-based and originate from a biological system. The same context as "Organic Chemistry." Organic used in this context does not refer to the agricultural practice of not using synthetic chemicals. This means that organic soil originates from natural materials like peat, coco coir, wood, compost, and other plant-based materials. These are typically mixed with materials like perlite or vermiculite that increase drainage and breathability.

Creating the Perfect Mix

The perfect potting mix can retain water all while providing adequate drainage and breathability. You want nutrient retention and a biological component that provides your plants with a probiotic matrix of healthy microorganisms. You ideally want something free of potential pathogens and seeds. Once you have all of your ingredients together you can place them on a large tarp and mix thoroughly.

Recommended Potting Mix
-50% Coco Coir or Peat
-25% Perlite or Vermiculite
-25% Compost, Activated Biochar, or both.

Peat Moss and Coco Coir

These two materials are used as the bulk for your soil mix and are useful in retaining moisture, providing air space, retaining nutrients, and serving as an overall good medium for your plant's roots.

Peat Moss is the most commonly used material in commercial soil mixes. It has a great ability to retain water, nutrients, and adequate porosity for drainage and air. While Peat retains twenty times its weight in water, it is also slightly acidic. When peat moss dries it also tends to acquire hydrophobic properties. It is not considered very biologically active meaning both micro and macro organisms do not feed on, consume, or decompose this material. While Peat Moss is commonly used in commercial soil mixes it is also considered an extremely nonrenewable resource.

Coco Coir is a renewable alternative to peat moss that has a much more minimal environmental impact. Coco Coir is produced by processing the fibrous husks of coconut that are a natural byproduct of coconut consumption. Like Peat, Coco coir is an incredibly good material for your containers because it has great water retention (absorbs up to ten times its weight in water) but also provides adequate drainage and breathability. It is pH neutral.

Perlite andVermiculite

Perlite and Vermiculite are inorganic (originating from the non-biological system) and serve primarily to improve drainage and air space while maintaining adequate water retention. Perlite is the white foamy granules you typically find in potting soils and has less water retention and more drainage compared to vermiculite. Vermiculite has a greater ability to retain water and nutrients when compared to perlite. Perlite is recommended for wetter climates, cactus, or more drought resistant plants. Vermiculite will be more helpful in arid climates, starting seeds, or for more moisture-loving plants.

Compost and Activated Biochar

These two materials are mainly added to add nutrients and a living biological component to the soil. Both these materials hold essential plant nutrients all while also feeding and providing habitat for the soil food web. This soil food web is crucial to maximize nutrient availability to your plants and protect them from pathogens.

The right compost is finely ground, homogenous, moist, and a dark color. Make sure its void of any material that is not fully decomposed, this suggests it was not processed fully or properly. Make sure it has a neutral smell and still has some moisture (not saturated) means that there is still biological activity present in your soil. Many people make compost nowadays, but it is not always done properly. This can lead to harmful soil conditions that can harm your plants or deprive them of important nutrients. They can also contain pathogens or unwanted seeds.

Compost will be mixed into your potting mix but can also be used as a "top dress" mid-season once your plant has grown in size and is beginning to flower. This top dress will slowly release nutrients down into the rootzone and help provide the necessary nutrients needed to produce fruit.

Biochar is essentially charcoal derived from easily renewable resources like bamboo, coconut husk, fast-growing wood, or a natural byproduct. Like in a charcoal filter, biochar acts like a sponge. It can soak up large quantities of nutrients and provide habitat for beneficial microorganisms. When freshly made biochar is mixed with a nutrient-rich substance (like compost or a nutrient-rich ferment) it absorbs all the nutrient goodness and becomes "activated." One of the most effective ways to do this is by soaking your biochar in a nutrient-rich liquid solution like liquid plant ferments, fish emulsion, urine, or nutrient-rich effluent. Biochar makes an incredibly powerful amendment that provides nutrients to your soil but also retains them and absorbs them when added through fertilizers. In larger pieces biochar has also been shown to share certain qualities with perlite and vermiculite.

Amending potting soil

Once you're done growing something in your potting soil it is very easy to bring more nutrients to your soil and return it fertility. Place your used potting soil in a tarp or bucket and mix with 15% compost or activated biochar. You can also amend it with a liquid fertilizer like compost tea but make sure not to oversaturate the soil.

Seeds and Transplants

Finally, you've come to need your plants! Whether you'd chose to start them yourself from seed or buy young starts, you must make the right decision in this choice. Ideally, start by finding a trusted and local provider. If you can find seeds or starts that were locally grown in your region, you know this variety can suit your climate and is better adapted.

If starting by seed, find fresh seeds, preferably packaged within the past five years because they will lose viability. Certain seeds lose viability quicker than others, the more recent they were packaged the better. Using viable seeds will save you a lot of time and effort.

If buying young starts make sure that they have an adequately developed but not overly developed root system. If a plant has been sitting in its pot for too long roots may become root-bound and will take longer to adapt to the transplant. Roots that have an inadequately developed root system will not be able to hold structure when transplanting and can cause major stress to your plants.

Organic and Conventional Fertilizers

Organic fertilizers are derived from all-natural materials like manure and vegetation. These are high in organic matter, slow release nutrients, and have little risk of damaging your plants. These can come in the form of compost, sea kelp, fish emulsion, compost tea or plant ferments Many of these also serve as great microbial inoculants that provide your soil with beneficial microorganisms.

Compost as a fertilizer
We've talked about adding compost into your soil mix, but it's also something that can be "top dressed" directly on the surface of your soil. Top dressing is a term for simply applying a surface level application of some amendment or fertilizer. Adding healthy compost to the surface of your soil will slowly move nutrients down into your root zone with every feeding and the natural work of diffusion and microorganisms. You can generously apply compost to your soil as long as you have room in your container, but it is best recommended to apply as your plants start flowering. You can also water your plants with a compost tea mentioned in the recipe below.

Easy Peasy Compost Tea Recipe
Ingredients; 4 cups of compost, 5 gallon bucket, compost tea bag, 5 tablespoons of unsulfured molasses, aerator or aquarium bubbler

To start, fill your bucket with water, ideally rainwater. If you're using tap water, you can choose to let it sit for 24 hours to allow the chlorine to evaporate for improved results. Leave about 6" to the rim of the bucket just to give you space to work with without spilling any contents. Mix in the molasses well. Put your compost in a compost tea bag (gunny sack or pantyhose work, too) and place it in the bucket. Turn on your aerator or aquarium bubbler and let it aerator for 24 hours. After 24 hours apply directly to your soil or as a foliar spray. Apply to your gardens early in the morning up to 2-3 times a week.

Kelp Fertilizer

Kelp Fertilizers are a great natural way for improving the performance of your plant. Kelp is essentially dried seaweed and is highly esteemed for its mineral and micronutrient content. It comes in the form of a powder or liquid which are typically diluted into water and used either in irrigation or as a foliar spray. The powder can also be top dressed or added directly to your soil mix. You can apply often in small doses, up to once every two weeks. Follow the instructions as indicated on your product.

Fish Emulsion

Fish emulsion is a natural fertilizer high in nitrogen and minerals that is derived from broken down fish. Be aware that this product is smelly! But it also is a powerful fertilizer. You dilute about half an ounce with one gallon of water and use for irrigation or spraying. It is best to be careful not to over concentrate your dilution because this can burn your plants. Apply once a week early in the morning.

Fermented Plant Juice

Plant ferments are fertilizers you can make at home by submerging green leafy vegetation in water with molasses. This liquid fertilizer is made by harvesting a large amount of soft herbaceous vegetation. Make sure to avoid sticks, anything woody, or dried brown leaves. Some good recommendations are comfrey, sunflower, squash foliage, mug wort, purslane, elder leaves, or any leafy green material. Break these down manually with loppers, a machete, shovel, or tool of your choice. Place these in a five-gallon bucket until 2/3 full and submerge with water. Add about one cup of molasses for every five gallons. Allow this to sit and ferment for about 2-3 months until vegetation is no longer recognizable. Strain into your final container. Apply about one cup for every gallon and apply 1-2 times per week.

Rock Phosphate

Rock phosphate is a phosphorus and mineral fertilizer that originates from ground phosphorus rich rocks. You will apply about 1-2 handfuls for every five gallons of soil in your garden once a year usually at the beginning of the season to reinvigorate your soil.

Conventional Fertilizers are highly refined nutrients which do not contain organic matter. They typically come in two forms; as a liquid or in solid granules. Conventional fertilizers are typically composed of three main nutrients that are typically the most limited in soil. These are nitrogen (N), phosphorus (P), and potassium (K). Check the packaging on your fertilizer for three numbers such as "10:15:10" which refers to the levels of each of these nutrients in the same corresponding order (NPK).

LiquidFertilizers

Liquid fertilizers act quick to provide the plant with easy access to nutrients. Liquid fertilizers can damage your plants if not properly applied on a more frequent basis. Try to avoid applying directly after transplanting as this can burn your damaged roots. Wait 1-2 weeks. To use, mix your fertilizer with water to the indicated dilution and use this liquid to irrigate your plants. Refrain from overwatering your plants in order to conserve fertilizer and apply once a week to heavy feeders.

Solid Granules

For most home gardeners it's recommended to use granular or slow release fertilizers because of the simplicity, effectiveness, and increased efficiency. Granular fertilizers are given to your plants in the spring before planting and often again during mid-summer for heavy feeders like tomatoes. These can be easily applied to the surface of your soil and with a little extra soil placed on top. Make sure to read instructions of your fertilizer brand before application.

Microbial Inoculants

Maintaining a healthy microbiology is one of the most important ways to have healthy, fast growing plants. These microbes come in the form of bacteria, yeasts, and fungi that all work together to reduce pathogens and make nutrients available to your plant. Creating healthy soil conditions is the most important part to having a healthy microbiome but introducing them to your soil can prove to be very beneficial in most cases. Introduction of these microorganisms is known as inoculation.

In most cases adding fresh good quality compost is enough to introduce these beneficial organisms to your soil. As mentioned earlier making an aerated compost tea is another easy way to inoculate your plants. Foliar sprays provide nutrients directly to your leaves but also coat your plant with beneficial microbes that ward off disease. Now at many garden centers you can find specific blends of microorganisms ready to go for inoculation.

Mycorrhizal inoculants are readily available in most garden stores and can improve the nutrient availability of your plants. These inoculants provide your plants with beneficial fungi that associate with their roots and increase nutrient access, repel pathogens, and make them more drought resistant. These will be important when first creating your potting mix and can be applied directly to the roots of a transplant or around a freshly planted seed.

Tools, Accessories, and Plant Supports

While so far, we have covered the basics of everything you will need to start container gardening, there are still several items that will make your life easier and increase the productivity of your plants.

List of Tools
-Hand shovel
-Tarp (for mixing soil)
-Watering container or hose with spray head
-Gloves

-Buckets for holding extra materials

-Pruningshears

-Scooping cups

Supporting Structures

Many plants do much better with additional physical supports that allow them to climb and spread vertically. There are different reasons why you would want to support your plants. Perhaps it's because they produce bigger yields like tomatoes or maybe they have a greater tendency to vine-like sweet peas. These structures can also maximize the growing space available by supporting plants to grow higher than they otherwise could on their own.

Stakes	Trellis	Cages
Garden stakes are great for tomatoes, eggplants, and chili peppers. These often require to be gently secured so they are properly supported.	Trellises are great for vining plants and can be made from many materials. Galvanized fencing works great for many projects. Lightweight plastic trellising can also be easily found.	Cages are good for spreading plants like tomatoes and chilies.
String trellis	**Hanging pots**	**Strings to your rafters**
String trellis is easily made by tying string to well-placed stakes. This works great with light climbers like peas and beans but can be risky with heavy producers like tomatoes.	While not technically a structure, hanging pots allow you to grow vines and other climbers without the need of a structure. Instead of growing up they can easily hang down from the pot.	Since you may be planting around your house, placing strings up to the rafters of your roof may serve as an adequate and convenient option for creating a structure.

Chapter 2: Plant Selection

From the aromatic sensation of fresh lavender to the sweet juicy flavor of a strawberry, cultivated plants are diverse and provide a different joy when brought into your life. For you, the greatest joy of gardening may come from nibbling on tart fruit fresh from your garden, or perhaps it will be making a sweet cup of fresh spearmint after a good meal. It might be preparing a fresh salad or harvest a bucket load of tomatoes destined for a sauce that you can use later in the winter. Whatever it may be, you are going to choose your plants based on whatever needs or wishes you'd like fulfilled. Secondly, you will need to find the right plants that are well suited to your climate, season, space, and the specific microclimate of your garden. You must also consider finding plants that are well suited for the specific size and location of your container. While certain plants are better suited outside of pots, others grow more vigorously than if planted directly in the ground. If you live in an area with a seasonal climate then you will also want to consider the timing of your planting and what time of the year would be best to plant what you are considering growing.

Plants for containers

Of course, not all plants are best suited for small spaces and container gardening. Thankfully there is a tremendously large choice of plants that do great in containers, some of which do even better in containers than directly in the ground. Plants not suited for containers are large trees and perennial shrubs that would not have adequate rooting space to properly grow in a container. Most annual plants, herbaceous perennials, and herbs are well suited for containers.

Annuals vs Perennials

Annuals are plants that typically live for one season and live less than a year. Some annuals may be an exception in tropical climates. Biennials live for two years. Perennials are long-lived plants that live for more than 2 years. You may hear the phrase long-lived perennial which refers to 10+ years.

Herbaceous vs Woody

Herbaceous plants are composed of rather soft and green vegetation. This includes anything from grasses to tomatoes. Woody plants are hard and typically acquire a brownish bark on their stems.

Plant	Light Requirement	Minimum Container Size	Cold Hardiness	Days Until Maturity
Arugula	Full Sun/ Partial Shade	1/2 Gallon	Winter	45-60
Bush beans	Full Sun	3 Gallons	Spring/ Summer	60
Beets	Full Sun/ Partial Shade	1 Gallon	Winter	60
Broccoli	Full Sun	5 Gallons	Winter	100-150
Basil	Full Sun/ Partial Shade	2 Gallons	Spring/ Summer	60
Carrots	Full Sun/ Partial Shade	2 Gallons	Winter	70-80
Cabbage	Full Sun/ Partial Shade	1 Gallon	Winter	80-180

Swiss Chard	Full Sun/ Partial Shade	1 Gallon	Winter	65
Collards	Full Sun	2 Gallons	Winter	60-85
Cucumbers	Full Sun	5 Gallons	Spring/Sum -mer	80
Carrots	Full Sun/ Partial Shade	5 per Gallon	Winter	80
Eggplant	Full Sun	5 Gallon	*Spring/ Summer	100-120
Kale	Full Sun/ Partial Shade	1 Gallon	Winter	60
Mint	Partial Shade	1 Gallon	Winter	50
Oregano	Full Sun	2 Gallons	Spring/Sum -mer	50
Parsley	Full Sun/ Partial Shade	1/2 Gallon	Winter	70-90
Green Onions	Full Sun/ Partial Shade	1 Gallon	Winter	30
Snow Peas	Full Sun/ Partial Shade	2-5 Gallons	Winter	70
Spinach	Full Sun/ Partial Shade	2 Gallons	Winter	45
Bell Peppers	Full Sun	5 Gallons	*Spring/ Summer	60-90
Hot Peppers	Full Sun	3 Gallons	*Spring/ Summer	150

Radishes	Full Sun/ Partial Shade	1/2 Gallon	Winter	22-70
Rosemary	Full Sun/ Partial Shade	2 Gallons	Winter	90
Squash	Full Sun	5 Gallons	Spring/ Summer	50-65
Turnips	Full Sun	1 Gallon	Winter	30-60
Tomato	Full Sun	5 Gallons	*Spring/ Summer	60-90
Cherry Tomato	Full Sun	2 Gallons	*Spring/ Summer	45-60
Zucchini	Full Sun	5 Gallons	Spring/ Summer	60-90

Winter-Plants can survive frosts and handle at least mild winters and may do better in warmer weather.

Spring/Summer-Plants do not like frost and prefer warmer weather.

*Spring/Summer-Plants prefer hot weather and do best when planted after the last frost in spring.

Considering your Space

One of the first things to consider before planting your container garden is the size of your space. You may want to maximize the number of things you are planting but make sure to consider that your space is adequate, and your plants are well-chosen to fill in an area nicely. You will want to position your plants so they can grow healthy and be productive while not being inconvenient or cumbersome. Consider leaving plenty of space to comfortably walk through your garden and have good access to your plants. You need to plant your plants according to their size, so they do not shade each other out and compete for sunlight and growing space. You can often "stack your pots" by having smaller and lower containers in front of larger containers oriented to maximize the sunlight they receive.

Things to Consider

Walls

Walls create shade and will have a drastic effect on the sunlight available. In the northern hemisphere consider that south-facing walls will often provide an environment with more sunlight than north-facing walls. Planting too close to walls can also crowd your plant and make it less accessible. Dark-colored walls will also absorb more sunlight while light-colored walls will reflect sunlight.

Other Plants

Other Plants may grow larger with time and shade out other plants. Plan according to the mature size of your plants and cut them back if you deem necessary.

Visibility

If some of your pots are not properly visible it's more likely they may receive less water and attention. Ideally, you want all the surfaces of your container to be visible.

Access

Make sure you have plenty of access to your containers so you can easily water and tend to your plants. If planting in a larger area, make sure to leave pathways between your plants so you do not damage other plants due to a lack of access. Try to place plants that are most often harvested from and require more attention in places you most frequent, like outside your door or the kitchen.

Water

Plants that are more dependent on water, should be placed with

---

closer access to water. Place these plants near your hose or where you fill up your watering can make watering these heavy drinkers easier.

Containers Can be Heavy
Once filled with soil and water containers can get heavy. While you are given the freedom of moving your containers, placing them well from the beginning will save you the hassle and risk of damaging your plants

Chapter 3: Planting Right

Most often what makes the real difference between a beautiful, productive garden and a mediocre one is the proper care and maintenance needed to have vigorous and happy plants. You can buy all the proper and most expensive materials, but if you're not there to give your plants routine feedings, fertilizers, and everything they need to thrive, they won't! Thankfully taking care of your plants is not a full-time job. It just requires a watering routine and occasional maintenance. With proper planning, your container garden will require much less work than a conventional garden while still being supremely productive.

Knowing Your Plants

Every plant is different. Some plants are adapted to the fierce cold winters of the north while others to the warm humid heat of the tropics. Some grow tall and lanky, some are vining, and some may be stout and low to the ground. Understanding the natural state of your plants is crucial to being able to properly provide conditions for it to flourish. For this reason, it's great to study the proper conditions, growth requirements, and living state of every plant that you wish to keep. Each will have their own watering needs, fertilizer routine, way of pruning, and even proper way of harvesting.

Using Intuition to Know Your Plants

Believe it or not, you don't always have to do an internet search or read a book to learn about your plant. Sometimes the plants themselves have morphologies and growing patterns that reflect the conditions they like. The easiest example is how leaf size correlates with its water and sunlight needs. Large leaves suggest the plant is adapted to more humid climates as is the case with bananas. Large leaf sizes have increased evaporation suggesting these plants are not limited by moisture. This could also indicate the plant does well in the shade, as many understory species have large leaves to capture indirect sunlight. Small leaves suggest the plant originated in dry conditions where it was hoping to reduce evaporation, as is the case with rosemary.

Proper Watering Practices

Establishing a proper watering routine is *essential* for maintaining a happy and thriving garden. As water is absolutely necessary to keep plants alive it's not something you can stop doing without having issues in your garden. While watering your plants is not exactly rocket science, there are best practices that will lead to the greatest results for your container garden.

Don't Over Water

Overwatering is probably the most common error committed by amateur gardeners. Overwatering can lead to reduced air space in the soil which makes your plant prone to root rot and other soil pathogens. When your soil becomes oversaturated it becomes what is known as "anaerobic" or lacking oxygen. This promotes anaerobic soil conditions that are harmful to the beneficial microorganisms you want in your soil. Also, if large amounts of water are draining through your pot then you are likely leaching nutrients and reducing the fertility of your container. Occasional deep watering is okay but must be infrequent.

Water Gently and Don't Make Pools

Along with not overwatering it is best to slowly administer your water to the container with low water pressure. You always want to apply water at an equal or slower rate to which it's entering your soil. If you add water at a faster pace than this, you will experience the water pooling on the surface of your soil which is rarely beneficial. You also want to make sure that the water gently hits the surface of your soil and does not cause it to splash up toward the foliage of your plants or disturb the soil too much. Disturbing the soil could expose

31

sensitive roots. Soil directly on the foliage of your plants could promote foliar diseases. I recommend putting a special head on your hose that allows you to go into a gentler spray mode or using a watering container with small holes. Avoid using buckets or directly from a hose.

Avoid Hydrophobic Conditions

It's not uncommon that at some point in time you will forget to water, and your soil will get severely dry. Perhaps you hadn't watered your garden for a while or there was a container you had routinely missed. Whatever the case is, it's important to take the right measure to remoisten the soil. The challenge occurs when soil dries up and gains hydrophobic properties that cause your soil to repel water. Thus, when you water, it all drains through the pot and is not properly absorbed. The best way to remedy this is with a saucer or tub. Place your plant in a saucer (if not already on one) or tub and water the plant. Notice if the soil is hydrophobic most of the water will drain right through and not absorb into the soil. Let the saucer or tub fill up 2-3 inches and wait 3-6 hours. During this time your soil will absorb this water from below due to the soil's natural wicking mechanism.

Occasional Deep Watering

Often the best watering routine for your plants is doing an occasional deep watering. In this process, you'll provide a deep watering to your plant's container until it starts draining from below. Then you must wait for the soil to almost dry out completely before watering again. This will encourage plant roots to expand and search for water. If you "pamper" your pot with constant water, your roots will not be encouraged to grow and will remain small. This weakens your plant giving it less access to nutrients therefore making it more susceptible to drought. While excessive leaching of your soil is unhealthy a small amount of water draining from your soil can actually prevent the buildup of mineral salts that can negatively affect the quality of your soil.

Don't Forget

While this seems obvious it's also extremely important. If you plan to leave on vacation during a hot dry season, make sure to have someone there to water your plants.

Self-Watering Systems for Your Plants

If watering your plants seems like a large commitment for you, then you should consider some self-watering options that automate this job. While many people enjoy watering their plants by hand it's completely understandable if you'd want to employ some time-saving strategies to automate this task. There are many ways to achieve a self-watering garden, each with many different pros and cons.

Drip Irrigation

While drip irrigation is something most commonly used in row crops, it's also a time and water-saving technology that can be applied to container gardening. Ideally to employ drip irrigation it's recommended you have large wide containers organized in a linear fashion, otherwise, the tubing can become messy and complicated. You can easily buy pre-made kits with everything you need or purchase all of your equipment separately. Drip irrigation is simple and easy to install once you familiarize yourself with its core concepts.

Drip Irrigation Equipment

1/2" Poly Drip Irrigation Tubing, Endcap, and Faucet
-This is the mainline hose that will attach from your faucet, it will run centrally around your garden.

Drip Irrigation Backflow Preventer
-Prevents water from being backfilled into your home's water supply.

Pressure Regulator
-Lowers the pressure coming from your faucet to prevent damaging drip systems.

Irrigation Micro Tubing
-Attaches to the mainline hose and delivers water to your pots.

Irrigation Timer
-Attaches in between your faucet and mainline hose which allows for automatization.

1 Irrigation Dripper with Spiker per Container
-The head that attaches to micro tubing where water comes out thus creating a spray.

Drip Irrigation Hole Punch
-Allows you to make holes in your mainline hose for attaching microtubing.

Drip Line Connectors
-Allows you to connect microtubing to the main line hose.

1/2" Tubing Stakes
-Stakes your tubing into a confined position.

Installing Drip Irrigation

1. Before you go and buy any equipment it's best to first take measurements, so you know exactly how many hose and pieces you need to buy. After you make your measurements, add an extra twenty percent just to be sure you have enough and for any future changes.

2. Simply attach the backflow preventer to your faucet, followed by the pressure regulator, the timer, and finally the faucet hose fitting at the end.

3. Attach your mainline hose and run it along your garden. Cut it at its final length and add the hose cap.

4. Connect your microtubing to the main hose by making a hole in the main hose with the hole puncher. Attach the connector and finally the microtubing.

5. At the end of the microtubing add the dripper spike.

6. Program the timer based on instructions of your specific unit and climate.

Self-Watering Containers

Self-watering containers are good options for low maintenance gardens. If you have a very busy schedule, leave home often, or just want to have a hassle-free garden this is a good option for you. These work by having a separate water container that is often located below or inside the hollow walls of a pot. Then a natural wicking mechanism, usually made of cloth or fabric, pulls water from the container into the pots. Many garden stores now offer prefabricated self-watering containers, but you can also easily make your own with readily available materials.

Make Your Own Self Water Container
Materials needed:
-A 5 gallonbucket with a lid
-Six 2" galvanized screws
-Water retentive cloth, fabric, old shirt, etc.

1. Start by cutting the rim off your bucket lid so it will fit in your bucket snug to the edges. You can drill ten holes directly into the lid evenly spaced. Make a larger hole 1" in diameter in the center
2. Drill your six screws into the side of the bucket 5" from the bottom and evenly spaced. Your cut out lid should be well supported by these screws.
3. Make 1/2" drainage hole in the side of the bucket 1/2" below your screws. This will help water drain if you overfill the water vessel.
4. Take a piece of fabric about 15" in length and 5" in diameter and roll it up lengthwise. Make a knot about 5" from the bottom of your rolled-up fabric, make sure the knot is bigger than 1 inch.
5. Place the fabric through the modified lid and place it in the bucket with the knot and along the side of the fabric on top.
6. Hold your piece of fabric up while filling your pot with the soil making sure it's in the center.
7. Water your container and extra water will drain down into the water vessel below. It will be absorbed by the fabric and naturally wicked up into your soil.

Starting Seeds

While you can easily find ready-to-go plants at a nursery you may opt to save a little money and have the full experience of starting your own seeds. Starting your own seeds can be greatly satisfying and allow you to produce a large number of plants for much cheaper than buying them at a nursery. Also starting seeds harvested from your previous harvests allows you to preserve good genetics which will make them more resilient to your local conditions. While it does have many upsides, starting seeds is a delicate process that requires attention and care to obtain good results. While you can start your seeds directly in your final container this can be cumbersome and more energy-intensive, so it's often recommended to start your seeds in smaller containers and then transplant them to their final home. This way you can keep all your young sensitive plants together and provide them with the extra care they need.

Consider Your Timing
You want to make sure to plant your seeds, so they have time to grow before the end of the season. If you'd like to get a head start in your season you can choose to start your seeds indoors before the last frost and then transplant them outdoors to your garden when the climate is more favorable. See the table below for minimum and optimal temperatures for the germination of selected plants.

Use the Right Containers
There are many different container options for starting seeds. You may choose to use small pots, plastic cups, plastic egg cartons, or other vessels you have lying around your home (make sure they have drainage). Otherwise, you may choose to buy prefabricated seedling trays. Prefabricated seed trays either come with individual cells of different sizes while others might just be one large tray. I recommend for most home gardeners to start your seeds in at least 2"x2" cells which will give them enough time to strengthen before transplanting.

Use the Right Soil
While the potting mix recipe shared previously would work well for starting seeds you can make it better by adding an extra fifteen percent of vermiculite. Vermiculite is more recommended than perlite for starting seeds because of its increased moisture retention.

Planting the Seed
Every plant has its own technique for planting. Make sure you familiarize yourself with this procedure and read the instructions if using a seed packet. Some seeds will be planted at a particular depth

while others are sprinkled on top. See the table below for the optimal depth of selected plants.

Watering

Watering with seedlings needs to be particularly gentle as to not overwater nor disturb the soil. It is best to do this with an airless sprayer or a pump sprayer with low pressure. Another great option is to fill your saucer or drainage tray with 1-2" of water and wait for it to wick its way up into the soil. Wait two hours and add more water if necessary. At the beginning phase, you need to be very careful that your soil doesn't dry out because young plants are not drought resistant. You may choose to cover your soil with a plastic sheet which will help retain moisture and slightly raise soil temperature. Make sure to remove this once the seeds have germinated.

Lighting

Make sure your plants receive adequate lighting. For indoor starting seeds that are near a window, flip your containers 180 degrees once every 1-2 days to prevent them from growing in one direction. For outdoor starting seeds, make sure the seed containers are well protected from heavy rain, either under an awning, greenhouse, or shade cloth. Shade cloths are particularly helpful in exposed locations as it will reduce evaporation and any stresses caused by intense sunlight. The mesh is also good enough to reduce the impact of rain.

Recommended Temperatures, Depths, and Optimal Germination Time for Starting Seeds

Plant	Minimum Temp Fahrenheit	Optimal Temp Fahrenheit	Germination Time (optimal)	Depth mm
Beans	60	85	6	30
Cabbage	40	80	4	6
Carrot	40	80	6	4
Celery	40	70	7	4
Corn	50	95	4	20
Cucumber	60	85	6	10
Eggplant	60	85	6	4
Kale	50	65	4	10
Lettuce	35	75	3	5
Okra	60	90	6	10
Pea	40	75	6	25
Pepper	60	85	8	5
Squashes	60	95	4	15
Swiss Chard	40	85	6	10
Tomato	50	85	6	5
Watermelon	60	95	4	15

Transplanting Tips, Tricks, and Things to Avoid

Transplanting is done once your plants have reached the maximum size for their pots and need more growing space. The term "up-potting" is used when moving a plant from a smaller container to a larger container. While transplanting is straightforward, some simple tips will help you minimize shocking your plants.

Make Sure Your Plant is Ready

Before transplanting anything into a new container make sure that your plant is ready to be transplanted. Fully developed roots will hold the soil into a solid structure. This means when you go to transplant, the soil root structure will be maintained. Avoid transplanting undeveloped plants because the soil may collapse and severely affect the root and soil's structure.

Massage Your Container

While it sounds a bit weird, massaging the outside of your pot with your hands will help remove plant roots from the sides of the container.

Loosen Root-boundPlants

A plant becomes root bound when it stays in a pot for too long causing the roots to completely take the form of the container. In this case, it's good to loosen these roots either by hand or with a knife so that they can better spread out into your new container.

Don't Pull Your Plants by the Stem

When transplanting, avoid pulling on the main stem to remove it from the container. This will damage the stem itself and its connection to the root system. With multi-celled trays this is necessary but just remember to be gentle!

Have Everything Ready

Make sure there is adequate space in your new container, apply any fertilizers, and your new container is accessible. Make a slightly wider hole with the same height as your previous container.

Hold and Flip

For medium containers, the best strategy is to place one hand on the bottom of the container and one hand on top with the stem going through your fingers. After having thoroughly massed your pot flip the container so the plant is upside down. Remove the container while still holding the root and soil structure in your other hand. If necessary, this is where you will loosen any root-bound plants. Place this in your new container and cover it with soil.

Companion Planting

To maximize your space and production you may choose to pair certain plants together that benefit from this companionship. By understanding your plants well, you can learn which plants may or may not grow together. Some plants are excellent ground covers, others grow straight and tall, while others are vines. Even below ground, plants take different structures of roots, some deep, some wide, and some mostly at the surface level. You can experiment with this if you feel comfortable in making pairings or gain inspiration from some of the most common companion planting guilds mentioned below.

Three Sisters

This is the most commonly heard of companion planting. It originates from the indigenous people of the Americas but can be applied to container gardening. This consists of planting corn, beans, and squash together in unison. You will need a large container at least 24" across and 12" deep. With a container this size, you can plant 6-8 corn plants evenly dispersed. Wait until the corn germinates and then place about ten beans around the germinated corn. Once the beans germinate plant one squash. The corn will grow tall and the beans will use it as a support structure. The squash will run horizontally and probably off your pot so make sure you have adequate space.

Tomato, Basil, Marigold

Tomatoes not only taste great with basil, but the basil can help repel pests when planted together. The marigold provides beautiful flowers but also helps deter root pathogens. Make sure to leave at least one foot between the tomato and other plants.

Leafy Greens, Carrots, Oregano

Leafy greens are often susceptible to pests because of their nutritious nature. Adding oregano along with your leafy greens will help repel any foliar pests you may encounter. Carrots will occupy a different part of the soil and will maximize your yield from your container. Make sure your container has at least one foot in depth to support the growth of your carrots so that you're not planting a leafy green that outlives your carrots.

Purslane Ground Cover

Purslane is a nutritious and tasty green that is rich in omegas. It grows independently and does not require much care. It naturally hugs the ground making it a great ground cover that will prevent the growth of weeds and add another crop to your space. Some other good grounded covers are Nasturtiums, French Sorrel, Strawberries, and Clover.

Chapter 4: Management of Pests and Plant Diseases

Even the best-kept gardens will at some point encounter pests and disease. While the best solutions are preventative, at some point you may have to take direct action to combat pests and disease. These are typically done through management practices that involve pruning, foliar sprays, pest removal, or restoring the health of your soil. There is a wide variety of pests and diseases so knowing how to combat your specific illness is crucial to winning the fight.

Most Common Causes of Pests and Disease

While healthy plants can be affected by pests and disease, those that are suffering from adverse conditions will be less likely to fight off serious issues and become more susceptible. Understanding what might be weakening your plants is crucial to finding a long-term solution to any issue you may be encountering.

Oversaturated Soil

Oversaturated soil is one of the most common causes of unhealthy plants. Not only will this promote the proliferation of unhealthy soil organisms, but it will starve your plants of oxygen and make nutrients less accessible. This can be caused either by overwatering or having insufficient drainage in your container. If you have insufficient drainage you can create more drainage holes from the bottom but if your soil is the core issue, this will be hard to remediate. In this case, your only option may be watering less or moving it out of the rain. Finally, make sure that you have a saucer or drainage plate to empty it more often or remove it altogether.

Overcrowding

If your plant is being overcrowded with its own or other vegetation, it can stress some of its foliage. Make sure your plant has plenty of space, sunlight, and is not overgrown. Some plants may require pruning so the foliage can breathe easily, and all leaves get adequate sunlight. Make sure to remove any diseased foliage. You can always move your pots further apart to promote more ventilation.

Undernourished

If you noticed your plant has stopped growing, become discolored, or is being affected by pests and disease it may be that it has run out of nutrients. In this case, giving your plants compost or fertilizers will help it tremendously. If your plant is rootbound you will see similar symptoms.

Under Harvested

Believe it or not, many plants do much better when routinely harvested. Harvest leafy greens like kale by harvesting the oldest leaves that will be most susceptible to disease. Remove infected foliage. Fruits like tomatoes will eventually become infected with pests if not harvested which will proliferate the infection of other fruits.

Temperatures

Every plant has its optimal temperature. If plants begin experiencing temperatures outside of their preferred range, then they will be weakened and may become infected. While this is hard to combat you may be able to find microclimates in your garden where they will be less affected.

Sunlight

While you will typically see signs of too much sunlight through limp and wilting plants, too little sunlight will often be seen in slow growth and infections. Make sure to double-check the light requirements of your plant.

Improper Pruning or Harvesting

Make sure you prune your plants with sharp and clean tools. Make sure your cuts are clean and at 45 degrees to prevent water from accumulating on the wound surface. For sensitive plants, you can apply charcoal to the wound to prevent any illness.

Understand the Vectors

Pests and diseases arrive from somewhere. It could be infected seed, soil, crop debris, nearby crops and weeds, dirty tools, or another source of cross-contamination.

Common Solutions for Treating Plant Pests and Disease

Neem Oil Spray
Mix 5ml of neem oil, 2ml of liquid soap, and 1 liter of water. Shake well. Works well against insects, fungi, and other diseases. To prevent fungi, spray susceptible plans once every two weeks and infected plants 1-2 times per week. Apply in the evening.

Soap-Water-Baking Soda Spray
Mix 1 tbsp of baking soda, 1 tsp of soap, and 1 gallon of water. Mix well until baking soda is dissolved. Helps fight against fungal disease. Apply to plants once every 1-2 weeks or after it rains. Apply in the morning so the solution has time to dry.

Soap-Water Spray
Mix 1 tablespoon of soap per quart of water. Mix thoroughly and use immediately. Works against aphids, whiteflies, psyllids, and mealy bugs. Apply every 4-7 days or as needed.

Diatomaceous Earth
Diatomaceous Earth is readily available at garden centers and helps control insects in the garden. Works against slugs, beetles, fleas, mites, and spiders. You simply apply it by sprinkling on and around your plants or wherever your pests occur. Apply after every rain or watering.

Bt
Bt is a common organic pest control made up of bacteria known as Bacillus thuringiensis (Bt is easier to pronounce). It is readily available in most garden

---

stores. It kills caterpillars and other soft-bodied pests. Apply every 7-10 days or as needed. Make sure to read the label for proper dilutions of the concentrated product.

Chili-Garlic Repellent
Blend 4 habanero chilis with 4 cloves of garlic and 1 liter of water. Strain and spray on your leaves affected by caterpillars. Apply every 3-4 days as needed or after rain.

Understanding and Treating Plant Disease

Just like us, plants are exposed to a large variety of microorganisms that live in their surrounding environment. Most of them are harmless, many are beneficial, and some can trigger an infectious disease. While plants, too, have an immune system that can fight off harmful infections they can also become ill and suffer the consequences. Understanding the nature of these diseases will help you understand the potential causes and how to apply the proper treatment. There are three main categories of disease; bacterial, fungal, and viral.

Fungal Disease

Around 85% of plant disease is caused by fungi and are some of the most difficult diseases to combat. Fungal disease can affect your stems, leaves, and even roots. Fungi are not just like the mushrooms on your pizza but come in a wide variety of forms many of which are microscopic. Fungi can be molds, yeasts, and rusts. They typically kill and consume your plant cells causing illness or even death. They can enter your plants directly through their leaves or by wounds caused by harvesting, insects, pruning, or any physical damage. Most commonly fungal diseases are caused by lack of ventilation, over-saturated soils, and the settling of water on plant surfaces. These can be easily avoided by moving your plants further apart, removing dead or sick foliage, watering in the mornings, and not watering the foliage.

Most Common Fungal Diseases and Treatment

Fungal Disease	Treatment
Powdery Mildew This disease manifests itself in many different plants as a white powdery coating on your stems and foliage. Affects melons, zucchini, lettuce, potatoes, parsley, pumpkins, grapes, peppers, and tomatoes. It often occurs if there is inadequate sunlight or airflow between your plants. It is not considered fatal but does reduce your plant's productivity.	Remove any diseased foliage. You can help treat powdery mildew with any of the following placed in a spray bottle and applied to your plants. One of the most common recipes is one tablespoon of baking soda, half teaspoon of detergent, and one gallon of water. A 3:1 mix of water to mouthwash has also been shown to be effective. Alternatively, many commercial treatment options are environmentally friendly and approved in organic gardening.
Downy Mildews Symptoms include discolored spots on the upper surface of leaves ranging from green, yellow, purple, or brown. Moldy growths on the lower surface of the leaf are also common. Effects: kale, peas, celery, spinach, cucumbers, pumpkin, cauliflower, mustards, and more. Often caused by water settling on the leaf's surface.	Remove any infected foliage as soon as any symptoms appear. Consider removing your entire plant if it's severely affected and neighbored by other potential hosts. Water in the mornings to give the plant time to dry during the day and avoid watering in the evenings. Difficult to remove once established the most recommended treatment is applying a copper-based fungicide.
Sclerotinia Rots Symptoms include water-soaked rotting stems or leaves and fruit that are slimy or smelly. This may be followed by the growth of white mold. Caused by cold and wet weather and contaminated soil.	Make sure your soil is not saturated and has sufficient drainage. Unfortunately, by the time this disease begins to show symptoms, there is little that can be done.

Black Spot Dark spots on the leaf's surface but not underneath. These grow until the leaf is yellow with black dots. These typically occur in the spring when temperatures are increasing. Most commonly affects roses, strawberries, and fruit trees.	Remove any infected foliage and make sure you have proper ventilation. Use the neem oil or soap-water-baking soda spray.
Gray Mold (*Botrytis cinerea*) First seen as a spot that appears water-soaked that then turns gray or brown. Can be seen anywhere on the plant but most often on leaves or flower buds. It can cause premature fruit to fall off. Typically occurs when humidity is high. Most commonly affects tomatoes, eggplants, potatoes, and peppers.	Make sure your plant has adequate ventilation and no water sitting on stems or leaves. Add mulch to your garden to prevent spores from splashing onto your plants from the soil. Attempt treating with neem oil spray. If neem oil spray doesn't work, then copper-based fungicides are an effective alternative.
Fusarium Wilt Fusarium is one of the most common and tragic plant diseases. This is easily identified because your plant will begin to wilt and is quickly followed by catastrophic wilting of your entire plant. It begins an attack on the roots and quickly follows up the vascular system preventing the transport of water.	Unfortunately, fusarium is incurable. Once your plant has begun to exhibit symptoms it's unlikely to recover and the fusarium will now contaminate your soil. Disinfect your soil by saturating your it with boiling water or placing it in a black plastic bag directly in the hot sun for two months. Add a microbial inoculant to your soil before planting.

Bacterial and Viral Diseases

While only about 15% of plant diseases are caused by bacteria or viruses, they still cause problems in most gardens. They are often caused by the same things as fungal diseases (overwatering, lack of airflow, excess humidity) but may require different treatments.

Most Common Bacterial and Viral Plant Diseases

Disease	Treatment
Black Rot It most often occurs in warm wet conditions and affects kale, cauliflower, arugula and mustards. Seen as yellow-brown v-shaped marks on vegetation that eventually dry up.	Remove dead foliage and unharvested fruit. Try applying compost tea early in the morning or the neem oil spray previously mentioned.
Bacterial Blight Occurs in cool, rainy, end of season weather. Seen as small brown spots on the leaf's surface that grow and can eventually cover the entire leaf	Remove infected foliage and prevent overhead watering. Try neem oil spray or a commercial copper-based fungicide.
Tobacco Mosaic Virus Tobacco mosaic virus infects tomatoes, eggplants, peppers, and tobacco. It causes a yellowing mosaic or streaking on the plant leaves. Veins will become yellow. Typically transmitted by other plants or cross-contamination of tobacco products.	Unfortunately, this disease cannot be treated. Remove all infected plants and do not save seeds. Avoid replanting anything susceptible in the same soil for at least two years.
Tomato Spotted Wilt Virus Effects tomatoes, peppers, potatoes, eggplants, lettuce, beans, spinach, cucumber, cauliflower, and others. Symptoms depend on hosts. Leaves will show small brown spots and will eventually die. New growth will often be the most affected and unable to mature. Sometimes plants will exhibit one-sided growth.	Remove infected foliage and make sure the plant has ventilation. This disease is caused by insects called thrips so removing them will be the first step in treatment.
Bean Blight Mostly occurring on beans and bean relatives. Displays symptoms with misshapen leaves, pods, and lesions on the plant. Typically spreads by	Remove infected vegetation but be sure not to handle it when wet as this may spread the bacteria. Dealing with beetles and whiteflies that spread the disease will be important in reducing

moisture.	its abundance. Copper-based sprays may help regulate it but will not remove it entirely.

Insect Pathogens

Not all plant pathogens are microscopic. Some of the most common pathogens you will encounter are insects. While some of these insects actively consume the vegetation of your plants, others plug into the vascular tissue of your plant and steal their sugar-rich fluids. Pathogenic insects will stress your plant resulting in slower growth and can also spread or promote other diseases. Making sure to treat insect diseases before they get out of hand is important to combat the threat.

Most Common Insect Pests and Treatments	
Insects	**Treatment**
Aphids Aphids are small sap-sucking insects typically 1/8" long. They typically occur on plant stems, leaf petioles, and around new growth. Aphids steal the sap from living plants often causing stunted growth, yellowing of leaves, curling of leaves, and can cause black, sooty mold. They also attract ants, so if you see ants on your plants check for aphids! There are several species and can range from green, yellow, orange, black, red, or pink.	You can start by knocking aphids off with water or by hand into a bucket with soapy water. Physically removing them is the best start. You will then follow up with a foliar spray of soapy-water or neem oil mix. Another option is introducing ladybugs that are known aphid predators.

Cabbage Worms Cabbage worms are the caterpillar of a small white fly that typically affects kale, broccoli, cauliflower, and other mustards. They are green and hairy with white spots along their back. They may be first noticed by the large irregular holes that they produce in your plant's foliage.	Like aphids, the best place to start is by removing the caterpillars directly. Look for eggs and remove those, too. You can apply diatomaceous earth on leaves or apply Bt. Another option is chili garlic repellent.
Potato Beetle About 1/2" long, yellow, and with distinctive black, brown, and yellow stripes on their wings. They lay yellow-orange eggs on the underside of leaves. They affect potatoes, peppers, eggplants, and tomatoes.	Remove all beetles, larvae, and eggs by hand. Make sure to dispose of them properly. Apply neem oil spray vigorously once every other day or as needed. Bt is also effective against larvae and can be applied daily as needed.
Corn Earworms Young worms that are mostly green, sometimes pink, with blackheads and they grow up to be 1 1/2" long. They attack fruit, most notably tomatoes, bean pods, and corn.	Adding vegetable or mineral oil on the silks at the top of the ear suffocates the worms. Neem and Bt spray are also effective but must be applied when silks have reached full size and are turning brown. Applying too early or too late will be ineffective.
Tomato Hornworms These caterpillars are about 4-5" long, bright green, and are common on tomatoes, potatoes, eggplants, and peppers.	Start removing by hand. Spraying with soapy water will make them wiggle and easy to see. Treat with Bt or neem oil spray.
Squash Bugs Squash bugs are shield-shaped with large antennae and feed primarily on squash, cucumbers, watermelons, cantaloupes, pumpkins, and other related plants. Squash bugs are gray with black legs and are much smaller.	Remove insects and egg masses manually. Apply neem oil spray or Bt. Laying a wooden board on the surface of your garden will attract stink bugs overnight. Remove in the morning along with bugs.

Controlling Pests and Disease to Protect Your Harvest

While infected plants will often continue living, they will most often have a reduced productivity or produce less nutritious and flavorful fruit. Remember that prevention is the key to treating these diseases and promoting adequate conditions for your plants will help keep any pests in balance. Remember that certain pests can appear if you're not adequately harvesting and consuming your fruits! If you have more than you can consume consider harvesting and processing them for use at a later time.

Chapter 5: Harvesting and Storing Your Bounty

After all your hard work and effort, the time to harvest your bounty has finally arrived. While it seems obvious, many amateur gardeners waste their efforts and the fruits of their labor because they lack the knowledge on when and how to properly harvest their crops. Just like planting and tending, harvesting also takes distinct knowledge of each plant to ensure you've maximized the quantity and quality of your harvest. Not only that but improper or lack of harvesting can damage your plant and reduce your potential harvest from that individual.

Finally, many gardeners are often overwhelmed by the sheer quantity of fruits and vegetables that their garden is producing and find themselves unable to consume the abundance of their production. For this reason, it's also very important to know how to properly process and store your harvests so you can use them at a future time when your garden is less abundant. In this chapter, we will go into great detail about the proper methods for harvesting, processing, and storing all the bounties of your garden!

Harvesting Your Bounty

While it may seem obvious at first, properly harvesting from your garden takes proper knowledge of each plant and their unique life cycles. Some plants, like most root vegetables, undergo a catastrophic harvest that kills the plant. If you harvest too late or too soon, you will find yourself not only diminishing the quantity of your harvest but also the quality. Other plants, like many leafy greens and herbs, are periodically harvested throughout their lifetime. Improper or lack of harvesting can cause damage to these sorts of plants or promote the development of pests that attack the fruits and vegetables that you intend to harvest. Knowing exactly when and how to harvest each plant is crucial to ensure you are getting the most out of your garden and making sure you get the most out of your efforts.

Top Tips for Properly Harvesting

Knowing When

Timing is essential. Knowing exactly when to harvest will ensure that you have the most flavor, best texture, and most nutritious fruit or vegetable. More often than not color is indicative for knowing when to properly harvest your plant of choice but usually takes a trained eye to see slight differences in color. While some fruits, like tomatoes, can properly ripen off the plant others will never ripen if harvested too early so, knowing if the ripening time has started is crucial. In contrast, waiting too long to harvest can impede the quality of your harvest because certain fruits like zucchini are more tender and appetizing when young. Not harvesting soon enough will also put you in competition with other bugs and critters that may start consuming your harvest!

Harvest Frequently

Some plants will often produce a larger quantity and better quality if they are harvested frequently. By harvesting kale, basil, and other leafy herbs frequently you will promote the production of new healthy growth and deter flowering. Infrequent harvesting of these plants will not only mean your otherwise harvested foliage may become infected and become prime real estate for pests, but an abundance of foliage can also trigger these plants to start flowering. While flowering is beneficial for fruit-producing plants, it can lead to less flavorful greens and end the life of certain plants earlier than necessary.

Use the Right Tools

With certain plants, the best tools to harvest are just your bare hands. With others you may want a sharp pair of scissors, pruning shears, or a knife to make clean cuts. Avoid damaging or ripping the stems of your plants when harvesting because this can be an easy entry point for pests and disease. Wash your hands and tools before you harvest because this too can lead to disease. Root crops are often easiest to harvest with a garden fork or shovel to help loosen the soil and ensure you don't damage or miss any part of your harvest!

Storing and Preservation

After your harvest, you will need to properly store your fresh fruits and veggies if they won't be eaten fresh. Certain crops like potatoes can be kept somewhere cool and dark for months while other things like tomatoes will go off within a couple of weeks even if refrigerated. Typically to extend the life of any harvest you will want to keep them somewhere cool, dark, and safe until they are to be used. If you wish to keep your harvest for months or potentially longer consider preserving your harvest in one of the following methods.

Drying and Dehydration

Drying your harvest is one of the best methods of preserving your fruits, vegetables, and herbs for long periods of time. It preserves and can even enhance their flavor and if properly stored makes them indefinitely shelf stable. This is because all of life needs water, so when you properly dry and remove all the humidity from your products you are making it uninhabitable for unwanted fungi, bacteria, or insects that would otherwise contaminate and compromise your products.

Many dehydrated products (like raisins) can be directly consumed in a delicious, lightweight, and easy to transport manner. Others can be rehydrated or directly added to your favorite dishes and used in a way comparable to the fresh products. Certain products, like herbs and some fruit, actually become more concentrated in flavor and will add a great kick to an otherwise simple meal! While certain things like beans can be directly dried on the plant in dry months others are not so simple. So how does one dry their farm-fresh products?

The easiest and most old-fashioned method is by laying them out in the hot sun. Any large juicy fruits or vegetables you will want to cut into smaller pieces or slices to maximize the surface area in which they can evaporate their fluids. Also, you may need to flip them routinely, so they dry out evenly. You can use a large metal baking tray that will absorb the heat of the sun and radiate it through your product. Alternatively, you can hang certain products like herbs or garlic by tying them together and hanging them with a string in a sunny area. Plastic mesh or metal screens can also be raised above the ground which will maximize the surface area exposed to the air and speed up the drying. If you need a boost you can place a fan in front of your set up to speed up the drying process. Always check that your product is crispy and dry before placing it in an airtight container for storage.

Unfortunately, if you live in a humid climate then drying in the sun can become complicated. You may in this case choose to purchase an electric dehydrator which can be as cheap as fifty dollars, build a solar dehydrator which will enhance your ability to use the sun, or you can even use your oven although this is typically energy inefficient and costly. To use your oven, place it on its lowest setting and place your products on a metal baking sheet inside. Allow it to heat up and routinely open the oven every twenty minutes for an hour. Then let it finish with the oven door slightly open to let out any humidity.

Canning

Canning is a simple and old-fashioned technique that involves storing your goods inside of glass jars that have been heated and sterilized. Sterilization is a process in which you destroy and remove any living organisms in your food that may cause it to start rotting, perish, ferment, or cause any undesirable flavors. You can do this with raw products, soups, sauces, jams, or almost anything you can think of! Canning is a great way to preserve food because it preserves the taste and quality of the food and is relatively cheap. Canned goods can last almost indefinitely if done and stored properly! There are two main ways to properly can. In a water bath or a pressure canning. Water bath canning is the simplest and can be done with materials you probably already own but is limited to acidic foods. Pressure canning requires a pressure canner but allows you to preserve any type of food.

Pickling

Pickling is a process of storing your harvest through fermentation in a salty brine or submerged in vinegar. Pickling in vinegar is the simplest method and done by submerging your product in vinegar inside a jar. The acidic environment created by the vinegar prevents the growth of any unwanted mold or bacteria. Making a salt brine will preserve and create an environment that favors microorganisms that are good for your health and repel any harmful microorganisms. Sauerkraut or Kimchi is a common type of fermented pickle. Pickled foods can often be preserved for several months or longer.

Tinctures

Tincturing is a process that involves extracting medicinal and aromatic components of herbs in alcohol for future use. This is simply done by taking any medicinal herb of your choice and soaking it in alcohol greater than 40%. After about one month you can then strain the liquid and have a shelf-stable extraction of the herbs of your choice. You can also mix and match herbs to create special medicinal formulas for any maladies you may experience.

Freezing

Often the easiest way to preserve your food is just freezing it! If freezer space is not an issue for you then this is a great option. Most fresh fruits and vegetables will become soft and squishy if defrosted so be aware of this! Frozen fruits are great for smoothies or making jams and jellies. Many vegetables will not be ideal for cooking once frozen unless you plan to use them in a sauce. A good way to freeze vegetables is by cooking them into a premade meal and then freezing the cooked food!

Chapter 6: Indoor Edibles

One of the great benefits of container gardening is that you now can garden indoors! Gardening indoors is fantastic because it brings a fresh green look to your space and can extend your season during cold winters. If you have highly valued perennial plants then you may choose to move them inside during cold months to protect them, promote growth, and improve their overall health. Growing indoors will also allow you to cultivate plants that prefer a dryer climate in wet conditions. In general, indoor gardening allows you to control the environmental conditions of your plants to better suit their needs and if well prepared can allow you to grow almost any crop in any weather!

What to Consider for Your Indoor Garden

Lighting: Light is the power that fuels the growth of your plants. Take time to assess the quantity of light in your indoor space and select the right plant for the environment. Most rooms will be limited by window space and thus only give you partial sunlight, meaning sun-loving plants won't do great indoors without additional lighting. Consider using shade-tolerant species or boosting your plants with artificial lighting. This can be done with specially designed grow lights, but regular house lights will also provide some additional lighting. Also, be aware that plants grow toward the light! If you're not using additional lighting directly above your plants be aware that they will grow toward your window or an artificial light source. You can counteract this if necessary, by rotating your plants 180 degrees away from the window.

Temperature: Depending on your climate and type of home or indoor structure temperatures will be drastically different. Unventilated structures in hot climates can become exceedingly hot and negatively impact the growth rate and health of your plant. In contrast, indoor gardening is great for cold climates because indoor spaces typically hold more heat than outdoor spaces, especially if your home is well insulated. Even still be aware that some homes and structures may not be insulated enough to prevent freezing indoors and that plants nearest to or touching windows will have a greater risk of being affected. If you wish to increase the temperature of your indoor growing space, you may want to consider supplying some extra light to your plants using incandescent or halogen lights that also produce heat.

Ventilation: If you are growing a large number of plants in a small or completely sealed space consider that you will want to ventilate the air. This will help reduce pests, promote the health of the plants and bring in the carbon-dioxide which is necessary for plant growth. This can be easily done by opening doors and windows or being as complex as building a ventilation system. Unless you are creating a high production and isolated grow room, ventilation systems are not necessary. You may also choose to ventilate to lower the temperature of your grow space.

Cleanliness: One of the first things people might think when growing plants indoors is, how clean is it to cultivate plants inside? If done properly your indoor garden can be clean, tight-knit, beautiful, and improve the air quality in your home. Of course, if not well managed than having an indoor garden can get messy, attract insects, and reduce air quality. If you have rambunctious pets or young children, then consider your indoor plants being at a higher risk of being tipped over and causing a great mess. Consider the sturdiness and placement of the surfaces your plants will be on. Cleaning up the soil in carpet flooring can be extremely tedious and difficult, while tile or ceramic is relatively simple to clean. Do not leave a large amount of dead foliage or decomposing organic matter in your home because this can create mold spores and attract insects.

Choosing the Right Plant: Not all plants are great for indoor gardening. Many of the most cultivated plants are not that great for indoor gardening because of light and space requirements. Large bushy plants can also attract more insects, be difficult to manage, and just look awkward in some spaces. The cleanest looking plants for your indoor garden will be small, stout, and compact plants as opposed to large bushy ones. Kitchen herbs are some of the first choices for many indoor gardens because it's always nice to have handy for cooking and they often take little space and have low light requirements. In chapter 8 we will cover many compact herbs that do well indoors and below we'll show you some other great crops for your garden.

Providing Ongoing Care: While maintaining an indoor garden is similar to any other garden, it does have its own distinct intricacies that make it a unique art form. It's important to start with well fertilized soil, so if you are reusing a previously used soil, add compost or the fertilizer of your choice. If you're starting with a fertile soil mix than you will not need any additional fertilization for the first eight to ten weeks of growth. Afterward apply an 8-4-4 fertilizer blend at 1.5 tsp per gallon every three weeks. Plants that are heavy feeders like tomatoes, eggplant,peppers, or squash should be topped off with compost as they begin to produce fruit. If your indoor growing space tends to accumulate a lot of heat during summer months, open your windows to provide proper ventilation. Unlike an outdoor garden it's important to water your garden frequently even during the rainy season! Depending on your plant and your climate you may need to water anywhere from 1-4 times a week. Check that the soil surface is dry before applying anymore water.

10 Easy Plants for Your Indoor Edible Garden

1. Sweet or Spicy Peppers

Crop Type: *Fruit*
Life Cycle: *Annual*
Sun Requirement: *Full sun/Partial shade*
Water Requirement: *2" of water per week or as needed to maintain moisture.*
Soil Amendment/Fertilizer: *Compost or 5-10-10 fertilizer*
Sow: *After last frost*
Harvest: *45-60 days*

Peppers are an excellent choice for an indoor garden because they can be kept relatively compact and will be protected from cold temperatures during the winter months.

How to Grow in a Container

-Start with seeds acquired from a pepper of your choice.

-Use a 3-5 gallon container. If starting from seed be sure to water the plant routinely as young seedlings are sensitive to drought.

-Choose a sunny window or give supplemental lighting for the best results.

-Once you see the first flowers on your plant, top off your container with extra compost to ensure good production.

What to Watch Out for

-Frail and sickly plants may have a viral infection, these are often spread by aphids and small insects.

-Root-knot nematodes are root pathogens whose symptoms manifest with chronically thirsty peppers.

-Large fruited varieties should be staked and tied to provide extra support.

Harvesting and Storing

-Simply pick peppers from the bush! Peppers can be harvested green for an earthier flavor or red for a sweeter and more robust flavor.

-Peppers can be dried, pickled, or incorporated into a tomato sauce and canned

-Spicy peppers can be preserved in a vinegar based hot sauce.

2. Radish

Crop Type: *Root vegetable*
Life Cycle: *Annual*
Sun Requirement: *Full sun/Partial shade*
Water Requirement: *1-2" a week or as needed to prevent soil from drying.*
Soil Amendment/Fertilizer: *Bone meal or any fertilizer rich in phosphorus and low in nitrogen.*
Sow: *Year round*
Harvest: *25-45 days*

Radishes are a great and quick crop for your indoor garden. They are particularly rewarding because they can often be harvested a month after planting!

How to Grow in a Container
-Plant radishes in a container 6" deep and as wide you'd like.
-Plant the seed 1/2" deep and with one inch spacing.
-Keep soil moist but avoid overwatering.
-You should see the top of the radish sticking out of the soil as it develops.

What to Watch Out for
-Warm weather can result leafy radishes which will not form bulbs.
-Do not let the soil dry out as it will cause the radish to boost, become pithy, and have a flavor too pungent to eat.
-Replanting radishes in the same soil will promote the presence of root maggots. Avoid this with proper crop rotation or incorporating a good quantity of wood ash to the soil.

Harvesting and Storing
-When the top of the radish is one inch across you are ready to harvest.
-Simply pull radish out from the soil and clean the root.
-Radishes are great preserved in a vinegar-based pickle.

3. Arugula

Crop Type: *Leafy green*
Life Cycle: *Annual*
Sun Requirement: *Full sun/Partial shade*
Water Requirement: *1-2" a week or enough to maintain soil moisture.*
Soil Amendment/Fertilizer: *Compost or 5-10-10 fertilizer*
Sow: *Late summer or early winter*
Harvest: *45-60 days after sowing*

Arugula is a great plant to keep indoors to have at convenience for making fresh salads.

How to Grow in a Container
-Plant in a 1/2 a gallon container near a north facing window. Cooler temperatures prevent arugula from bolting and extends their lifespan. During the winter when there is less day light hours, move container to a sunnier south-facing window.

-Sow seeds at 1/4" deep about 4" apart or broadcast seed and thin when plants are about 1" tall. To thin, simply cut unwanted plants at soil level with sharp scissors. These young thinned plants go great in salads.

What to Watch Out for
-Don't overcrowd your plants as this will promote foliar diseases.

-Remove infected plants and organic debris from the soil to reduce the prevalence of diseases.

-Avoid wetting foliage as this can promote the growth of downy mildew. Symptoms of this include brown spots on the tops and bottoms of leaves.

Harvesting and Storing
-Pick leaves from the outside of the plant after 30 days and cut any flowers to extend the growth season.

-Arugula is best used fresh but can be stored in the refrigerator for 1-2 weeks.

4. Broccoli

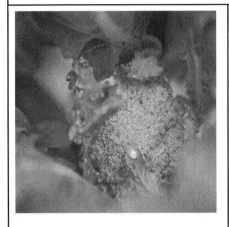

Crop Type: *Vegetable*
Life Cycle: *Annual*
Sun Requirement: *Full sun/ Partial shade*
Water Requirement: *2-3" a week or as needed to maintain moisture.*
Soil Amendment/Fertilizer: *High nitrogen fertilizers like compost or 10-5-5 fertilizer.*
Sow: *Year round*
Harvest: *100-150 days*

Broccoli is an excellent and productive indoor plant, particularly during cooler times of the year.

How to Grow in a Container
-Broccoli requires a good amount of soil so use a 5 gallon container per plant. Sow seeds approximately at a quarter inch of depth into the soil and provide 3 feet of growing space per plant for the production of a large head.
-Keep in a sunny location with 6 hours of direct sunlight or provide supplemental lighting with grow lights.

What to Watch Out for
-Slow growth likely suggests that your plant isn't receiving enough sunlight. If this is the case move to a sunnier location or provide supplemental lighting.
-Control gnats by placing of small bowl of apple cider vinegar with water and a drop of dish detergent.

Harvesting and Storing
-Once your broccoli head is of good size it is ready to harvest!
-Broccoli can be kept for 1-2 weeks in the refrigerator or cut into chunks and pickle in vinegar.

5. Swiss Chard

Crop type: *Leafy green*
Life cycle: *Annual*
Sun requirement: *Full sun/Partial shade*
Water requirement: *1-2" a week*
Soil amendment/fertilizer: *Compost or nitrogen rich fertilizer*
Sow: *Spring-Autumn*
Harvest: *45-60 days*

How to Grow in a Container

-Use a container 6" deep and plant seeds 1" deep and 3" apart. Water gently so as to not disturb seeds in the soil.

-Plant will not need fertilizer for the first month of growth and may not need any for 2-3 months if placed in a large container with fertile soil.

-Start fertilizing once growth slows down with a nitrogen rich fertilizer. Top dressing with compost is usually enough as chard is not a heavy feeder.

What to Watch Out for

-Avoid wetting the foliage as this can promote diseased leaves with irregular brown marks.

-Warm dry weather will result in reduced vitality for your plant and may mean the end of the season. Sickly plants should be removed and replaced with a summer crop.

Harvesting and Storing

-Harvest chard by cutting the larger outer leaves with a sharp knife or scissors. Leave young growth for future harvests.

-Chard is best used fresh from the garden. You can also choose to cook and freeze it for later use.

-Dehydration is suitable for adding into soups but the texture is not equal.

6. Kale

Crop type: *Leafy green*
Life cycle: *Annual*
Sun Requirement: *Full sun/Partial Shade*
Water requirement: *1-2" a week or as needed to maintain moisture.*
Soil amendment/fertilizer: *Compost and 10-10-10 fertilizer.*
Sow: *Fall or Early winter*
Harvest: *30-60 days after sowing*

Kale is an excellent choice for your indoor garden because it's a handy compact green that goes great raw in salads or cooked in countless dishes.

How to Grow in a Container
-Grow kale in a 1 gallon pot near a sunny window.
-Sow 1 plant per container as they will grow large in size and compete with each other if planted too close.
-Start harvesting the lower leaves after about 30 days and do so regularly to prevent flowering.

What to Watch Out for
-Keep an eye out for caterpillars and remove them immediately.
-Kale prefers cooler climates so it might not be the best choice during hot months.
-Aphids and white flies can be treated with water-soap-baking soda spray or neem spray as indicated in the pest management section.

Harvesting and Storing
-Use fresh in salads or cook into any meal.
-Dry or bake until crisp in the oven makes for great kale chips!
-You can cook and freeze kale to be incorporated into a future meal.
-Lasts for 1-2 weeks in the refrigerator.

7. Green Onions

Crop Type: *Leafy green*
Life Cycle: *Annual*
Sun Requirement: *Full Sun/Partial shade*
Water Requirements: *1-2" a week*
Soil Amendment/Fertilizer: *Start with composted well-draining potting mix and add 5-10-10 fertilizer if growth slows.*
Sow: *3 weeks before last frost*
Harvest: *40-50 days after sowing*

Green onions are versatile and great in any savory meal, cooked or fresh!

How to Grow in a Container
-Use 1-2 gallon pots, the wider the better as green onions only need about 8" of soil depth.
-Fill pot 2/3 full of soil and place bulbs root side down 2" apart. Fill the remainder of the container to bury bulbs.

What to Watch Out for
-Keep near a sunny window where plants receive 4 hours of direct light or consider supplementing with artificial lighting.
-Watch for black and yellow insects that leave a thin white trail on your foliage. These are leaf miners and can greatly decrease yield. Manage this by removing infected plants immediately.

Harvesting and Storing
-At around 6" of height the plant is ready to harvest. You can either remove or consume the entire plant, or simply cut the foliage leaving the bulb in the ground. The latter option will allow the foliage to continue growing and allow for future harvests.
-Will last for 2-3 weeks in the refrigerator.
-Store in a vinegar-based pickle.

8. Ginger

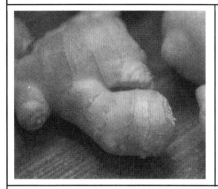

Crop Type: *Root vegetable*
Life Cycle: *Perennial*
Sun Requirement: *Partial shade*
Water Requirement: *2-3" a week or as needed.*
Soil Amendment/Fertilizer: *Add compost 6-8 weeks after planting.*
Sow: *After last frost*
Harvest: *100 days*

Ginger is a tropical species that can benefit from indoor cultivation in cooler temperate climates.

How to Grow in a Container
-Ginger is grown from the ginger root that you are familiar with. It can be started from store bought organic ginger.
-Take your ginger root and cut into 1-2" pieces and let these pieces dry out for 2-3 days. This allows the fresh cuts to dry and reduce the chance of infection.
-Plant these about 4-6" apart and 1" deep. Ginger does not have particularly deep roots but use a wide pot 8" deep.
-Foliage should sprout within 2 weeks.

What to Watch Out for
-Ginger likes warm climates so it may do best during summer months.
-It may take a while to sprout but makes sure to keep watering your container even if it seems like there is nothing growing!

Harvesting and Storing
-Once the foliage starts turning brown you know it's time to harvest. Pull up the vegetation and search through the soil for the ginger roots.
-Ginger can last for several weeks unrefrigerated if left in the open air in a relatively dry environment.
-It can be stored for long periods of time in a vinegar-based pickle
-Drying ginger is also a great option but it may lose intensity of flavor. Dried ginger can be ground into ginger powder.

9. Spinach

Crop Type: *Leafy green*
Life Cycle: *Annual*
Sun Requirement: *Full sun/ Partial shade*
Soil Amendment/Fertilizer: *1-2" a week or as needed to maintain soil moisture.*
Soil Amendment: *Add compost or 15-10-10 fertilizer after 8-10 weeks.*
Sow: 6 weeks *before the last frost*
Harvest: *30-60 days*

Spinach is a great leafy green to grow indoors. It is compact and extremely versatile.

How to Grow in a Container
-Plant spinach in a 1 gallon container with your common potting mix no closer than 6" apart.
-Keep near a sunny window preferably with morning light.

What to Watch Out for
-Dark speckled discoloration on the foliage is the result of rust. Manage this by removing any organic debris from the container or replace plant with a rust resistant variety.
-Aphids, caterpillars, slugs, and other leaf eating insects can be common in spinach. Treat with neem oil spray 1-2 times a week or as needed.

Harvesting and Storing
-Harvest after plant has 8-10 large leaves, harvesting older leaves first.
-Use fresh in salads or mixed into any cooked dish to add a healthy dose of green protein!
-It can be stored in the fridge for 1-2 weeks or cooked and frozen for later use.
-Dried spinach can be incorporated into soups or green smoothies.

10. Garlic

Crop type: *Root vegetable*
Life cycle: *Annual*
Sun requirement: *Full sun/Partial shade*
Soil amendment/fertilizer: *0.5" to 1.5" a week or as needed.*
Soil amendment: *High nitrogen fertilizers like compost, blood meal, or a 15-10-10 mix.*
Sow: *Year round*
Harvest: *100-150 days*

Garlic is an easy plant for beginners and requires little space making it an excellent choice for an indoor garden.

How to Grow in a Container

-You plant garlic using the garlic clove you are familiar with from cooking. If using store bought garlic make sure to use organic garlic for better results.

-Use a pot 8" deep for adequate root growth.

-Place your cloves 1" deep and 4" apart.

What to Watch Out for

-Chose a south or west facing window that provides 6 hours of direct sunlight or supplement with artificial lighting.

-Don't peel cloves before planting! This outer skin is important to protect the clove from pests!

Harvesting and Storing

-Once almost all your leaves have turned brown you know it's time to harvest.

-Dig up bulb by gently digging around the base of the plant until you expose the bulb. Carefully remove the bulb and brush off excess soil without bruising the cloves.

-You can hang your garlic in a dry location, and it will last for several months or freeze for an extended period.

-Dried garlic makes a great addition to your spice cabinet but is less flavorful than fresh garlic. A dry powder can be mixed with salt to make garlic salt.

-It makes a great condiment when pickled in vinegar.

Chapter 7: Balcony/Patio/Rooftop Gardening

Urban agriculture is something that is becoming more common throughout the world as a means for city dwellers to reduce their environmental impact and promote food security in times of an uncertain future. While you may feel like your small city apartment is not proper for starting a farm, it's likely that you can still grow high quality produce in the little space you may have. Outdoor spaces like a balcony, patio, or even your rooftop can actually be highly productive spaces if properly planned and maintained. For many, these outdoor spaces are an important place to relax, socialize, and get fresh air, so adding a bit of green will also provide a pleasant natural ambience to the setting.

General Preparations and Practical Considerations

Adding a garden to your urban space can be a satisfying feat that provides fresh food and a beautified environment to spend your time. While space is usually a limiting resource in these settings, a well-designed and creatively adapted garden can host a wide variety of productive plants. Understanding your options for utilizing the most out of your space and sunlight hours are crucial to properly designing these outdoor garden spaces.

Lighting

What you'd first have to consider when designing your balcony, patio, or rooftop garden is the hours of sunlight that you have available in this space. If your outdoor space is on the southern facing side (in northern latitudes) of your building and is not obstructed by other buildings or trees, then you might almost have the full sun accessible to your growing space. In contrast a northern facing balcony or one obstructed by other buildings, structures, or trees will be much more limited in light, thus limiting the types of plants you can grow.

East facing spaces will have morning sun, which is suitable for many crops, while west facing spaces tend to have afternoon and evening sun. It's important to consider and observe how much sunlight you have before investing in any particular type of plant.

Spacing

Once you've figured out your available lighting, you will have to determine what crops are suitable and how you plan to fit them into your space. Considering the size that these plants reach in maturity will help you choose their proper location, making sure that they won't shade out or have to compete with other plants in your garden. For example, while it might make most sense to have sun loving plants near the front of your balcony garden, many plants grow big and bushy and thus may shade the rest of your garden. Instead you may choose to plant plants that stay smaller near the front and planting large plants that require larger pots near the back. This way you have a tiered placement where smaller plants will not compete with larger plants. At this point you will also want to consider accessibility to all of your pots, as you will need to harvest, water, and do occasional maintenance to each of your crops. The great thing about container gardening is that you can always move and organize your pots as your understanding of the space and plants evolve!

Creative Strategies for Maximizing Space

There are also many creative solutions and tools you can use to maximize your grow space. Vertical planters can be hung on your walls giving you not only easy access to your plants but also utilizing otherwise empty wall space. Stacked pots allow you to place more plants into smaller spaces without interfering with space and sunlight. Companion planting as was discussed in chapter 3 is also another good strategy to maximize limited space. Hanging pots from either the roof or your railing can also provide a nice look and utilize otherwise unused space.

Strawberry pots are also practical space saving containers that are ideal for many smaller plants. These are usually tall pots with staggered openings around the outside walls that provide multiple places for planting. While traditionally used for strawberries these are also great for many small herbs or plants.

10 Easy Plants for Your Balcony, Patio, or Rooftop Garden

1. Tomatoes

Crop Type: *Fruit*
Life Cycle: *Annual*
Sun Requirement: *Full sun/Partial shade*
Water Requirement: *2-4" per week*
Soil Amendment/Fertilizer: *Compost and high phosphorus fertilizer or a 5-10-10 amendment*
Sow: *Beginning of spring*
Harvest: *60-90 day*

A store-bought tomato will never compare in flavor to a homegrown one! If you have adequate space and plenty of sunlight, then tomatoes will make a great choice for your outdoor space.

How to Grow in a Container
-Tomatoes require plenty of nutrients and potting soil so, use at least a 3-5 gallon container to achieve good growth and production.
-Start your seeds in a seedling tray or small pot to save space while plants mature, try to keep soil temperature at 70-75 degrees Fahrenheit.
-As the plant begins to flower, give additional fertilizer in the form of compost tea or a 5-10-10 blend and continue feeding every 2-3 weeks.
-Most tomatoes will require some form of support. Start with a central pole and a cage for bushy varieties, while vining varieties can be grown up your railing or any form of fencing. Cherry tomatoes can vine up strings connected to your roof.

What to Watch Out for

-Consider your variety of tomato. Some are determinant and have short lifespans while others are indeterminate and live until they die of cold temperatures or other stressors. Some are bushy while others, like cherry tomatoes, grow in a more vining pattern.

-Aphids, white flies, potato beetles, and horn worms can be naturally treated by spraying neem or Bt. Manually removing insects/eggs and spraying dish soap mix can help but will be more labor intensive and may not help with heavy infestations.

-Powdery mildew and other fungal diseases on leaves can be treated with conventional copper sprays.

-Yellow mosaic discoloration could be tobacco-mosaic virus. In this case it's recommended to get rid of the plant immediately to prevent its spread and not to plant peppers, potatoes, or tomatoes in this same soil for 2-3 years.

Harvesting and Storing

-Tomatoes are often best when left to ripen directly on the vine, turning a classic red with most varieties.

-If you're having an issue with pests attacking your tomatoes, you can harvest green as soon as you start seeing a change in color and let them ripen safely in your kitchen. Green tomatoes are also edible if cooked.

-To harvest, hold the stem with one hand and pull the fruit with the other. Avoid ripping the stem tissue as this can promote disease.

-Canned tomato sauces make an excellent option for storing tomatoes. Drying them is possible but difficult due to its high water content.

2. Onion

Crop Type: *Root vegetable*
Life Cycle: *Annual*
Sun requirement: *Full sun/Partial shade*
Water requirement: *1-2" a week or as needed*
Soil Amendment/Fertilizer: *Compost and nitrogen rich fertilizer like 15-10-10 mix.*
Sow: *Year round*
Harvest: *45 days*

How to Grow in a Container

-Plant by seed in a container at least 8" deep with plants 3-4" apart.

-You can broadcast seed and thin them out as plants mature, harvesting the young thinnings for cooking.

-Preferably use a well-draining soil mix with extra vermiculite.

What to Watch Out for

-Avoid having excess decomposing organic material like leaves or mulch, this may attract slugs that may also consume your onion.

-Small white lesions might be leaf blight, in this case thin your plants and provide better air circulation.

-Downy mildew appears as pale spots or even grey purple fuzzy growth on the leaf's surfaces. Leaves will turn pale to yellow and have collapsed leaf tips. You may try treating with a baking-soda spray and if that doesn't work then a fungicide may be your only option. Avoid planting other onions or garlic in this same soil.

Harvesting and Storing

-Dig up onions from the ground and wash off any excess dirt. Hang and keep in a breezy, dry place until the necks are completely tight, dry, and the tens contain no moisture.

-Pungent onions (like the ones that make you tear up) can be stored for up to a year if stored in a dark cool place. Otherwise store onions in acidic salsas, chutney, or caramelize and freeze.

3. Carrots

Crop Type: *Root vegetable*
Life Cycle: *Annual*
Sun Requirement: *Full sun/Partial shade*
Water Requirement: *1-2" a week*
Soil Amendment/Fertilizer: *Low nitrogen fertilizer like 5-10-10 mix.*
Sow: *Early spring, 4-5 weeks before last frost date.*
Harvest: *70-90 days*

How to Grow in a Container

-Use a container is at least 8-12" deep and full of well aerated soil.

-Plant by sprinkling the seeds on the surface of the soil. Afterward take about a handful of soil and sprinkle them above the seeds. Once seeds germinate thin them so there is 1-2" of space between each plant.

-Feed carrots with additional compost or a 5-10-10 liquid fertilizer every three weeks.

What to Watch Out for

-Many different types of diseases in carrots are caused by insects which transmit the disease. If you notice leafhoppers, caterpillars, or beetles on your foliage immediately treat them with neem or Bt.

-Do not replant carrots in the same containers as this will greatly increase your risk of disease.

Harvesting and Storing

-Grab carrots by their tops and pull up the entire carrot! If they seem like they're still undeveloped, leave them for another 2-3 weeks.

-Pickling carrots is a great way to preserve them and makes a nice snack.

4. Sweet Peas

Crop Type: *Fruit*
Life Cycle: *Annual*
Sun Requirement: *Full sun/Partial shade*
Water Requirement: *1-2" a week.*
Soil Amendment/Fertilizer: *Low nitrogen fertilizer like potash or 5-10-10 mix.*
Sow: *Fall or spring*
Harvest: *60-90 days*

How to Grow in a Container
-Use a container at least 6" deep and wide enough to space plants 4" apart.
-In places with mild winters you can plant in the fall and grow through the winter. Otherwise they are best planted in 45 days before the last frost date in spring.
-Plant seeds about 1.5" and 4" apart.
-Sweet peas are vines so providing a structure for them is important. You can use tall wooden stakes, chicken wire, or the railing of your balcony. Tying strings to your roof is also a great option.

What to Watch Out for
-Watch for aphids that commonly attach to the stems and underside of leaves in sweet peas. Spray with neem or dish-soap spray and physically remove them from your plant.
-Avoid planting in containers that previously had beans or other legumes to reduce risk of diseases.
-Dead spots, translucent patches or white streaks on leaves could all indicate a viral infection. These cannot be treated with organic or chemical controls. Avoid replanting legumes in this container.

Harvesting and Storing
-Harvest by hand or use a pair of scissors to gently remove them from the vine. Hold the vine steady with one hand when picking to avoid damaging the brittle stem.
-Tender green pods can be eaten fresh and go great in salads or even cooked!
-The young growing tips are edible and go great in a stir fry.
-As the pod becomes woodier or yellow you must harvest it and open it to remove the edible pea.
-You can dry the green pea and rehydrate when ready for cooking.

5. Strawberries

Crop Type: *Fruit*
Life Cycle: *Perennial*
Sun Requirement: *Full sun/Partial shade*
Water requirement: *1-3" a week*
Soil amendment/fertilizer: *Pre-fertilized, soilless media amended with compost or a slow release fertilizer like 10-10-10.*
Sow: *Spring*
Harvest: *120 days*

How to Grow in a Container
-Starting traditional varieties from seed can be difficult and time consuming. It's recommended to buy bare root or potted plants in the spring. Alpine varieties can be easier to grow from seed.
-Plant in container 8" deep with 2-3 gallons of fertile potting mix.
-Fertilize every 2 weeks with high potash fertilizer after 45 days of growth.
-Consider growing alpine varieties for shadier spaces and your common garden strawberry in sunnier places.

What to Watch Out for
-If your plant is not producing fruit, but plenty of flowers, you may have to hand pollinate! Grab a dry and clean paint brush, and hand pollinate the flowers by brushing the center of the flower.
-Strawberries love occasional coffee grounds but it's not recommended to give more than 2 tbsp of coffee grounds every 2 weeks!
-Many fruit loving insects may come and devour your strawberries before they're even ripe! Place diatomaceous earth around your plants to protect them.

Harvesting and Storing
-Avoid pulling the berry as this may damage the plant. Instead gently cut or snap the stem.
-It is best to harvest berries in the morning and immediately refrigerate.
-Do not wash until right before consumption or use.
-Extra strawberries can be dried or made into jelly or preserves.

6. Lettuce

Crop Type: *Leafy green*
Life Cycle: *Annual*
Sun Requirement: *Full sun/Partial shade*
Water Requirement: *1-2" a week*
Soil Amendment/Fertilizer: *Nitrogen rich compost and 10-10-10 fertilizer*
Sow: *Spring-autumn*
Harvest: *40-60 days*

How to Grow in a Container

-Lettuce needs cool temperatures below 77 degrees Fahrenheit to germinate, so plant accordingly.

-Sprinkle lettuce seed in a container at least 5" deep and cover with about a quarter inch of soil. Water lightly so as to not disturb the seed and soil too much.

-Seedlings appear in a week or two, thin them to be 3" apart when they are about 2" tall.

-If your potting mix was made with nitrogen rich compost or a slow release fertilizer, then feeding is not necessary. If your soil fertility is questionable or your container is smaller than 2 gallons per plant, then feed every 2 weeks with a 10-10-10 or any general-purpose fertilizer.

What to Watch Out for

-Caterpillars causing foliage damage. These creatures should be physically removed from the plant. Check under and around damaged leaves.

-Watch out for slugs that will eat your greens! Physically remove them and use an iron phosphate-based bait around the plant if they continue causing problems.

-Brown spots or mildew on foliage may be caused by excessive moisture on leaves. Avoid wetting the foliage and water in the mornings to reduce any foliar diseases.

Harvesting and Storing

-There are two types of lettuce; those that form a tight heart and those with loose leaves. The tight heart varieties like romaine are usually entirely harvested about 45 days after plating. The loose-leaf varieties can be harvested various times in their life by only cutting off the leaf tops and allowing new leaves to regrow.

-Remove the bottom leaves of tightly packed varieties because they tend to be dirty and often more diseased.

-Lettuce is best eaten fresh but can be stored in the fridge for 1-2 weeks.

7. Green Beans

Crop Type: *Fruit*
Life Cycle: *Annual*
Sun Requirement: *Full sun/Partial shade*
Water Requirement: *2-4" a week*
Soil Amendment/Fertilizer: *Compost and 10-10-10 fertilizer*
Sow: *Spring/summer*
Harvest: *60-90 days*

How to Grow in a Container
-Use a container that holds at least 4-5 gallons of well fertilized potting soil.
-Place seeds about 5 seeds 1" deep and 5" apart.
-Climb plant onto balcony railing or a trellis of your choice.
-You can also hang the plant down from a hanging basket.

What to Watch Out for
-Avoid wetting the foliage as this can lead to foliar diseases.
-Don't leave your bean pods on the plant for too long as they will turn woody, harbor pests, and may become infected.
-Dark blotches or lesions on stem may be caused by a fungus known as anthracnose that occurs in wet conditions. There are no cures to this but avoid wetting the foliage to reduce its virulence.
-Sclerotina fungus will form watery spots on leaves and cause your stem to rot. It will also cause your bean pods to become soft. This is caused by cool, moist conditions and can be improved with better air circulation. Alternatively, it means it's the end of the season and time to remove the plants.

Harvesting and Storing
-Simply remove bean pods when they are still tender so they can start becoming plump.
-You can leave the pods to dry on the plant during summer to have dry beans for rehydrating at any time of the year.
-Pickle green beans in vinegar to preserve them.

8. Beets

Crop Type: *Root vegetable*
Life Cycle: *Annual*
Sun Requirement: *Full sun*
Water Requirement: *1-2" a week*
Soil Amendment/Fertilizer: *Compost and phosphorus rich fertilizer like a 5-10-10 blend.*
Sow: *Spring-autumn*
Harvest: *70-80 days*

How to Grow in a Container
-Choose a container at least 10" deep and place seeds 1" deep and 3" apart.
-Feed with a phosphorus rich fertilizer 35 days after planting and continue to do so every week until harvest.
-Small varieties like the "baby beet" or the "baby gold" are best for containers.

What to Watch Out for
-Irregular or round brown marks on foliage may be a fungal disease known as Ramularia. This can be prevented by not wetting the leaves, watering in the morning, and providing more warmth and sunlight. Otherwise conventional fungicides are your only option.

Harvesting and Storing
-Beets can be harvested by simply pulling them up by the base of the leaves. If for some reason your soil is compact, use a small gardening shovel for support.
-Beets can last for several months stored in a cool dry place, like a cellar.
-Pickling beets is a great way to preserve them and enhance their flavor. The pickled juice is great for making dressings and other colorful sauces.

9. Eggplant

Crop Type: *Fruit*
Life Cycle: *Annual*
Sun Requirement: *Full sun/Partial shade*
Water Requirement: *2-4" of water a week or enough to maintain soil moisture.*
Soil Amendment/Fertilizer: *Start with well composted soil and add 5-10-10 fertilizer every 2 weeks during fruit production.*
Sow: *After last frost*
Harvest: *120 days*

Eggplants are great indoor plants especially in cooler climates where they struggle outdoors. If given a large enough container, sufficient space to grow, adequate sunlight, and extra fertilization, they can produce well inside in most climates.

How to Grow in a Container
-For best results plant individually in a 5 gallon container near a sunny window.
-Eggplant requires a temperature of 68F for germination. Plant at least 2 seeds per hole when directly sowing into the container as they may not all germinate. Thin out the weaker looking seedling if you have two sprouts.
-Once your eggplant starts producing add 2-3 heaping handfuls of compost to your soil surface and continue doing so every month for better production.
-While they are considered annuals, it's not uncommon that they live for more than a year if properly maintained.

What to Watch Out for
-If you notice flea beetles on your plant immediately treat by spraying Beauveriabassiana or spinosad. If left untreated, they can completely wipe out your plant.

Harvesting and Storing
-Harvest eggplants when they turn purple.
-Once they begin turning brown, they become less tender.
-Eggplant can be stored in refrigerator for 1-2 weeks.
-You can grill or cook eggplant and freeze for later use.

10. Cucumbers

Crop Type: *Fruit*
Life Cycle: *Annual*
Sun Requirement: *Full sun*
Water Requirement: *2-4" a week*
Soil Amendment/Fertilizer: *Compost and high potash fertilizer*
Sow: *Spring/summer*
Harvest: *80-100 days*

How to Grow in a Container
-Choose a container that can hold at least 5 gallons of soil.
-In a wide 5 gallon container, you can have 2-3 plants but the more plants the more feeding and maintenance is necessary.
-Plant seeds 6" apart or more and plant 2-3 seeds per location. Three to four days after germinating, choose the most vigorous one and thin the others by cutting with scissors at the base.
-Cucumbers are climbers. Place near your balcony railing or make a trellis from chicken wire or wooden stakes.
-You can top dress with compost as flowers begin to appear. If you have more than one plant per 5 gallons of fertile soil, feed with a nitrogen rich fertilizer twice a week.

What to Watch Out for
-If your flowers are not producing fruits you may need to hand pollinate! Female flowers have a small bump in the shape of an immature cucumber at the base of the flowers that will be absent in male flowers. Take the stamens of the male flower and rub into the female flowers.
-Remove any dead or dying plant material as this can harbor a white mold that can become pathogens on the cucumber's vegetation.

Harvesting and Storing
-Once fruits are firm they can be harvested with a knife or pruning scissors.
-Cucumbers can be stored in the fridge for about 10 days.
-Store for a long period of time as pickles. Season with dill to make the famous dill pickles!

Chapter 8: Herb Gardening

Herb gardening can be one of the most satisfying and impactful forms of gardening from a culinary perspective. The aromatic sensations created by the foliage of many herbs enriches the flavor of foods and make for excellent teas. Many of these herbs also hold medicinal properties that can relieve the symptoms of many common ailments and lead to an overall healthier lifestyle. It is also one of the easiest ways to garden because most herbs are long lived perennials that are easy to propagate and require little attention. Herb gardens are often great to have indoors on a windowsill or right outside the kitchen for easy access.

Where to Plant

What you'll have to consider first when designing your herb garden is the sunlight and temperature requirements of every herb. Most can be grown year-round on your windowsill while others may have preferred seasons or will be more productive outdoors. Many fragrant aromatic herbs are derived from dry climates, particularly those with small or white fuzzy leaves like sage, lavender, thyme or rosemary. These thrive in full sunlight but are still highly productive in the shade. In contrast many cool seasons thrive best in the shade when exposed to less sunlight. Some examples of are spearmint, parsley, and cilantro. It's also good to consider seasonal requirements for certain plants, for example basil thrives best in the heat of the summer while cilantro enjoys the cooler weather of spring and autumn. For this reason, it's important to understand the requirements of every plant in order to determine their best location and when to plant them.

General Principles of Herb Gardening

If you want to invest the least amount of energy for the maximum effect, herb gardening is often the best way to go. Most herbs are relatively low maintenance perennials, meaning that if they're well looked after the same plant could live for years in the same pot. While relatively simple, there are some general principles to follow when starting your herb garden.

Containers and Soil Essentials

Most herbs grow best in well-draining soils that are kept moist but not over saturated or completely dry. Make sure to use a well-draining but water retaining potting mix as described in previous chapters and avoid using sediment based "backyard" soil. Check your containers for proper drainage holes and if using a saucer or drainage plate make sure to empty it after watering. The size of your container largely depends on the plant you are cultivating. Large perennials like rosemary will thrive best in pots that are at least 1 gallon in size, while small annual herbs do good in pots as smalls 8" in diameter. Plants in smaller pots will often benefit more from frequent fertilizing as they'll run out of nutrients in their soil sooner than those in large pots.

Water Wisely

The watering needs of your herb garden partly depends on the container size, the plant, and the climate. Smaller containers and large leafy plants typically require more water, especially in hot or dry climates. In contrast large containers or small woody plants require much less water, especially in humid or cold climates. In general, most indoor containers will require watering every two or three days. A good procedure is watering when the top inch of soil dries up. In extremely hot and dry climates you may need to water up to twice a day, especially for smaller containers.

Feed Lightly

Unlike fruit producing plants, most herbs actually require little fertilization. Excessive use of fertilizers can damage your plants and result in poor flavor even if there is more production of foliage. Most plants will thrive for long periods of time without fertilizers if planted in rich potting soil, but the fertilizer requirements depend on the particular plant. Most herbs will be happy with a balanced soluble fertilizer, diluted up to 1/4 of the package recommended rate, applied every three weeks.

Pruning and Harvesting

Like many plants harvested for their foliage, foliar herbs often produce more when they are frequently harvested or pruned. Cutting back foliage can also extend the life span of many herbs and prevent them from outgrowing their pot or becoming diseased. Some plants, like basil, will often benefit and have an extended life span from a drastic pruning up to more than half of their foliage. Other slower growing herbs like rosemary and thyme should be harvested in less quantity, typically no more than fifteen percent of their total foliage. Perennial herbs should also be harvested and pruned less in the winter when growth is slower as this can shock the plant. Herbs harvested for their flowers or seeds should usually be untouched until they produce their blooms and have their seeds fully developed and dried. Cleaning and disinfecting your shears or scissors will greatly reduce your risk of disease and keep your plants healthier for longer!

Getting Creative

Herb gardens not only make pleasant aromatic sensations but can also make beautiful features to your home. Placing herbs in stylish pots on your kitchen window is convenient and pleasant to the eye. You can even plant herbs in old kitchenware like colanders, bowls, mugs, or jugs to play with the theme of your kitchen.

Mason jars can be used for planting herbs by filling the bottom 1/3 with large rocks followed by a coffee filter and soil. The rocks allow for water to drain and not stagnate in the soil, while the coffee filter will prevent the soil from washing into the rocks. This method will also allow you to watch the roots grow and make a fun project for young kids!

A suspended shelf made with recycled wood and rope can also make a great support for herbs that will allow you to use the full length of your window. A short step ladder can also make a great shelf and provide a creative way to support a variety of pots. You can also make hanging jars by tying a rope around a potholder and hang it from your ceiling! Since most herbs don't require much soil, it's easy to fit many herbs into small spaces and up-cycle old equipment into shelving or containers!

10 Herbs for Your Home Garden

1. Oregano

Life cycle: *Perennial*
Sun requirement: *Full sun/Partial shade*
Water requirement: *1-2" with well-draining soil*
Soil amendment/fertilizer: *Light, well-drained, moderately fertile soil. Prefers a soil pH of 6.0 to 7.0*
Sow: *Spring*
Harvest: *Not recommended to start from seed*

How to Grow in a Container
-Oregano can be started from seed but may be quicker through cutting of an established plant or buying a nursery start.
-Use a container 6" deep and replace ever 2-3 years when the plant becomes woody and has outgrown the pot. Use a container 2x the size when transplanting.
-Sow seeds a quarter inch deep and 6" apart.
-Feed oregano by spraying with compost tea or liquid sewed extract once every 1-2 months during the growing season.

What to Watch Out for
-Oregano will die back in winter and will reshoot in the spring, so don't worry if your plant is looking sickly during the beginning of the winter. You can bring the plant inside to extend its season.
-Oregano growing in over-saturated soils may suffer from root rot.

Harvesting and Storing
-Harvest growth as needed once the plant is at least 4-6 inches tall. Constant harvesting will result in fresh growth and better production. it is best harvesting with garden clippers or sharp scissors by snipping fresh growth.
-Flavor is best before plant goes to flower.
-Dehydrate and store in an airtight container.

2. Rosemary

Life Cycle: *Perennial*
Sun Requirement: *Full sun*
Water Requirement: *1-2" a week in well-draining soil*
Soil Amendment/Fertilizer: *Vermiculite, compost and a nitrogen rich fertilizer*
Sow: *Spring*
Harvest: *Purchase seeds or starter plant from a nursery and harvest when the plant is at least 6" tall and bushy from spring to autumn*

How to Grow in a Container

-Rosemary is best grown from a young plant as starting from seed or cutting can be time and energy intensive. You can find young plants in most nurseries, year-round.

-A 1-2 gallon pot is typically enough for a small rosemary bush. Use a container at least 2-3x in size to promote new growth.

-Encourage fresh growth by trimming rosemary several inches twice every season after the flowers have faded.

What to Watch Out for

-Rosemary is rarely affected by pests but mealybugs and scale may harm stressed plants. You can remove scale by wiping it off with an alcohol-soaked cotton ball.

-Rosemary is susceptible to root rot in wet climates. Amend soil with compost and avoid growing plants too close together.

Harvesting and Storing

-Occasional harvesting is beneficial to the plant and done by harvesting 4-6" springs of fresh growth from the tips of branches. Strip individual leaflets from the stem. Avoid pruning more than 1/3 of the plant at a time because this can stress the plant.

-Air-dry your rosemary and store in an airtight container or freeze for future use.

3. Culinary Sage

Life cycle: *Perennial*
Sun requirement: *Full sun*
Water requirement: *1-2" a week in well-draining soil*
Soil amendment/fertilizer: *Vermiculite, compost and a nitrogen rich fertilizer*
Sow: *Spring*
Harvest: *Purchase nursery start and harvest when the plant is bushy. Avoid winter harvests*

How to Grow in a Container
-Its recommended to start culinary sage from a rooted plant because starting from seed or cutting takes a long time and a lot of energy.
-A 2 gallon pot is enough for a small sage bush. When transplanting, use a container at least 2-3x in size to promote new growth.

What to Watch Out for
-Water in the morning and avoid wetting the foliage to prevent foliar diseases.

Harvesting and Storing
-Harvest leaves from established plants using garden shears or sharp scissors. Keep sage bushy by pruning 6-8" of growth twice during the growing season.
-Harvest from late spring to autumn and avoid winter harvests as this can stress the plant.
-Dried sage stores well in an airtight container and can be ground up for easy use.

4. Mint

Life Cycle: *Perennial*
Sun Requirement: *Partial shade*
Water Requirement: *2-3" a week depending on variety, size, and location.*
Soil Amendment/Fertilizer: *Compost and nitrogen rich fertilizer*
Sow: *Spring*
Harvest: *60-80 days from cutting*

Mint is a great plant to keep indoors so you can easily harvest and prepare yourself a tea when tempted. It's great to consume after a large meal or when feeling nausea or any stomach discomforts. Avoid companion planting with mint as it will take over!

How to Grow in a Container

-Mint is best planted from a rooted plant or cutting. You can often remove a rooted cutting from an already developed patch. Keep soil moist as the plant develops.

-Mint will do great in containers as small as one gallon but requires more fertilization in smaller containers.

-Plant several rooted cuttings as close as 1" apart to more quickly colonize the container.

What to Watch Out for

-If growth slows and leaves start to lose their color apply a nitrogen rich fertilizer every two weeks and top dress with compost.

-Remove any dead growth and harvest frequently to promote new growth.

-Fungal diseases can occur when plants become over watered.

Harvesting and Storing

-Harvest by cutting fresh lanky sprigs that are at least 6" long with sharp scissors near ground level.

-Harvest routinely to promote new growth. Never harvest more than 20% of young plants and give them time to regrow. Once plants have fully developed into your container, you can harvest almost the entire plant to promote healthy new growth and ward off disease.

-Drying mint works well and intensifies the flavor. Keep in an airtight container.

5. Basil

Life Cycle: *Annual*
Sun Requirement: *Full sun*
Water Requirement: *2-3" in well-draining soil*
Soil Amendment/Fertilizer: *Compost or nitrogen rich fertilizer*
Sow: *Spring after last frost*
Harvest: *90-120 days*

Fresh basil is an essential ingredient for almost any Mediterranean or Italian classic dish. If grown properly it can be extremely productive and one of the greatest staples in your garden.

How to Grow in a Container
-Basil can do fine in a 1-2 gallon container but will grow bigger and more vigorous with 3-4 gallons of soil.
-Plant at least 8-12" apart if planting a large container.
-Prune back flowers routinely to extend their growing season.

What to Watch Out for
-Water in the morning and avoid wetting foliage to reduce any foliar diseases.
-Slugs are also a common enemy of basil. Visit your plant at night and physically remove snails. Placing eggshells and ash around your plant can also help.

Harvesting and Storing
-Harvest basil by cutting off long lanky growth that is at least 6" long. Cut back basil flowers below the first node along with two side branches.
-Basil is best used fresh and loses much of its aromatic properties when dried. Making an oil-based pesto is often one of the best options when it comes to preserving its freshness!

6. Thyme

Life Cycle: *Perennial*
Sun Requirement: *Full sun*
Water Requirement: *1-2" a week with well-drained soil.*
Soil Amendment: *Vermiculite, compost and a nitrogen rich fertilizer.*
Sow: *2-3 weeks before last frost.*
Harvest: *2-3 weeks before the last spring frost*

Thyme is a sun loving, Mediterranean herb that can thrive on a sunny windowsill. It adds excellent flavor to a variety of dishes and sauces.

How to Grow in a Container

-It is best to start from cutting from an established plant because seeds take a long time to establish. Start cuttings indoors 6-10 weeks before last frost.

-Use a container that is at least 6 inches deep.

-Move container indoors or to protected area during winter months.

-Prune plants in the summer and spring if overgrown.

What to Watch Out for

-Thyme will grow better if fed with a nitrogen rich fertilizer twice a month from spring to autumn. This is particularly important after the first year of planting.

-Thyme is adapted to dry conditions so, it's imperative to avoid overwatering.

Harvesting and Storing

-Once plants are 6-8" tall cut leaves with garden scissors as needed, leaving tough woody stems.

-Flavor is best before thyme begins to flower. For drying this is the best time to harvest.

-Fresh thymes lasts 1-2 weeks refrigerated.

7. Lemongrass

Life Cycle: *Perennial*
Sun Requirement: *Full sun*
Water Requirement: *2-3" a week*
Soil Amendment/Fertilizer: *Compost and nitrogen rich fertilizer*
Sow: *Spring after last frost*
Harvest: *60-90 days from root bulb*

Lemongrass makes delicious medicinal teas and is a crucial ingredient in Asian cuisine. It is grass and native to tropical climates but can be grown seasonally or moved inside through the winter.

How to Grow in a Container
-Lemongrass is grown from the bulbous base of the grass which can be dug up from a developed plant or bought from the grocery store. You can also find it in many nurseries already developed.
-If starting from store-bought stems, then remove the outer layer of stems and root in water. Transplant into a container at least 1-2 gallons in size after 4 weeks when roots have developed.

What to Watch Out for
-Lemongrass originates from a tropical climate so it's best to bring plants indoors to a sunny location when temperatures start to drop.

Harvesting and Storing
-Harvest leaves once leaves are 1-2 feet in size and the plant has grown at least 4-5 new shoots. Cut the grass about 4" from the base from which it will regrow.
-Lemongrass is best consumed fresh as its flavor will not last when dried.

8. Parsley

Life Cycle: *Bi-annual*
Sun Requirement: *Full sun*
Water Requirement: *2-3" a week*
Soil Amendment: *Compost or nitrogen rich fertilizer*
Sow: *Spring after last frost*
Harvest: *80-90 days from seed*

Parsley is a pungent herb that adds great flavor to salsas, pasta, and a variety of dishes. The leaves are not only flavor enhancing but highly regarded as nutrient rich and medicinal.

How to Grow in a Container
-Parsley can be planted individually in 1-2 gallon containers or you can have several plants spaced at least 8-12" apart in a larger container.
-Start fertilizing after 45 days of growth. Do this by top dressing with compost every month or using a nitrogen rich fertilizer every two weeks.

What to Watch Out for
-Parsley lives for two years, making its flower in the second year. Second year foliage is bitter and not as pleasant.

Harvesting and Storing
-Parsley is ready for harvest as soon as leaf stems have three segments.
-Leave inner portions of the plant to mature and harvest from the outside of the plant.
-You can keep parsley by placing stems in a cup of water and placing in the refrigerator.
-You can dry parsley just by hanging it in the shade in a ventilated area if the climate permits. Once it's crumbly, store in an airtight container.

9. Cilantro

Life Cycle: *Annual*
Sun Requirement: *Full sun*
Water Requirement: *2-3" a week*
Soil Amendment: *Compost and nitrogen rich fertilizer*
Sow: *Spring after last frost*
Harvest: *80-100 days*

Cilantro is easy to grow and is what adds the extra kick to any salsa or ceviche. The seeds are also commonly consumed as coriander.

How to Grow in a Container
-Cilantro grows great in containers 8-10 inches deep and 18 inches wide.
-Sow seeds a quarter inch deep, 3-4" apart, and keep soil moist until germination.
-If starting in a seed tray, transplant once they have devoted 2-3 leaves.
-Fertilize about once a month with liquid fertilizer or use slow release pellets. Soils well amended with compost may not need fertilization.

What to Watch Out for
-Keep plants well-watered to prevent the plant from bolting and going to seed early.
-It does not do well in cold or wet climates so move inside at the beginning of winter to prolong its season if it was planted late.
-Dark brown or black spots on the foliage may be a fungal disease worsened by wet weather. Prevent wetting the foliage to reduce the risk of this disease.

Harvesting and Storing
-Harvest after about 60-70 days of growth by cutting some stems from the base with sharp scissors.
-Flowers and seeds are also edible and make great seasonings.

10. Chives

Life Cycle: *Perennial*
Sun Requirement: *Full sun/Partial shade*
Water Requirement: *1-2" a week*
Soil Amendment/Fertilizer: *Compost or nitrogen rich fertilizer*
Sow: *Spring*
Harvest: *60-90 days*

Chives are an easy way to add an oniony flavor to any meal. They grow easily on a windowsill and can live for many years with little maintenance.

How to Grow in a Container
-Chive plants are small so they can be grown in containers as small as a coffee mug. Use a container 6" deep and as wide as you'd like.
-If starting from seed, sprinkle the seed over your soil followed by a sprinkle of soil just enough to lightly cover the seeds.
-If starting from a developed plant, separate the individual bulbs and evenly disperse these in your container about 1/2-1" apart.
-Apply fertilizer or top with compost about once a month during the growing season.

What to Watch Out for
-Chives are resistant to most foliar diseases but can be prone to root rot in water-logged soil.
-Avoid overcrowding in areas with high humidity as this can cause fungal diseases to develop.

Harvesting and Storing
-Feel free to harvest as soon as you have a large enough clump and your container seems full. Just cut the foliage 2-3" from the base.
-The flavor of chives is not preserved with dehydration. Making chive butter or oil is an excellent way to preserve the flavor for a longer period of time.

Chapter 9: Growing Micro

Microgreens are the newest and easiest superfood you can grow at home! They're gaining popularity around the world because of their nutrient rich properties and unique flavors that add a special kick to any meal. Microgreens are essentially the young seedlings of crops that would otherwise grow into mature plants given the time. They are quick, easy to grow, and require little maintenance when compared to growing full-size plants. Since microgreens grow mostly from nutrients already stored in the seed, they don't require fertilization and since they grow so quick, they don't really suffer from pests or disease! They are great for topping off salads, dips, or adding into any sandwich. They also can add a nutritional boost to any shake or smoothie!

Everything You Need to Know to Grow Your Own Microgreens

If you've ever germinated a seed and grown it to a seedling, then you've essentially grown a microgreen! The difference is that since your intention is not to grow a mature plant, you can plant the seeds much denser and harvest within 2-3 weeks. Most of your well-known herbs and leafy greens are great for growing as microgreens and are a great crop for tiny indoor spaces! There are two options for growing microgreens; either traditionally with soil or hydroponically. Some plant varieties have a preference, but both are easy and yield good results. You likely already have all the materials necessary for doing it with soil, so you can start like this and move on to a hydroponic system if you choose!

Material for Growing Microgreens

Seeds

Seeds are the most important part for growing your microgreens. It's important to acquire high quality seeds, the fresher the better, as to ensure a good germination rate. If you want a good harvest of microgreens you will need hundreds of seeds, so buy in bulk or from large seed providers intended for microgreens.

Soil

If using soil, you can use your common potting soil but adding an extra 15% vermiculite or perlite to create better conditions for seed germination. You can also find ready-made seed starting mix at most garden centers. Some sources will recommend using vermiculite to top your container off after planting seeds, but this is optional.

Hydroponic Grow Matt and Nutrients

Alternatively you can purchase Hydroponic grow matts for microgreens that will remove soil from the equation. These grow matts are just soaked in nutrient amended water and then placed in your common 10"x20" propagation trays. Use a general hydroponic nutrient that is available at most garden centers where hydroponic equipment is sold and use as directed.

Container for Microgreens

Since you will not be growing a full-sized plant, your microgreen containers don't need much depth. Two to three inches deep is all you need to grow most microgreens! You can grow in containers as small as silicone muffin cups or use large seedling trays for a larger crop. Just make sure your container has sufficient drainage and place a saucer or water retaining container below it to catch excess water. Avoid large containers as you will be wasting soil and space! For hydroponic cultivation most matts are designed to fit 10"x20" propagation trays.

| **Light Watering Container or Spray Bottle** |
You will want a small watering can with a very fine nozzle that gently and accurately releases the water. Most watering containers are not accurate enough nor gentle enough to not disturb the soil. You can find specialty watering containers for microgreens, use a spray bottle, or even make your own from a plastic water-bottle.

Microgreen Basics

Microgreens are extremely simple to grow, and most varieties can be grown using the same basic principles. Some seeds can be soaked to speed up the process and ensure better germination results. Depending on the size of the seed planting density may also vary.

1.Choose Your Space

Microgreens don't require much space and can easily be grown on a windowsill, outside, or even beneath a grow light. Certain seeds do require certain temperatures for germination, and most will germinate quicker in warmer temperatures. During winter months you can purchase a warming mat to help speed up the process. As long as your containers receive some sunlight your microgreens will do just fine.

2.Prepare Your Container

If using soil, make sure your container has adequate drainage and is at least 2-3" tall. Fill your container with your seed starting mix and leave a 1/4" of space between the top of the soil and the rim of the container. Make sure you have a water retaining saucer or tray to place your container in.

Alternatively, you can use a hydroponic matt that is designed to fit a 10"x20" propagation tray. These are also known as 1020 trays. Soak your matt in water that's amended with hydroponic nutrients then drain and place in your tray.

3.Sow Your Seeds

Sprinkle your seeds densely but make sure they are all in contact with the soil or grow matt and not on top of each other. Gently press them down into the soil or matt. As previously mentioned, some seeds must be soaked before planting. For soaking simply leave in cold water for 12-24 hours in your fridge. Drain, rinse, and use as directed. Typically, you will use 1-1.5 oz of seeds for a 10x20" propagation tray.

4.Black Out Period

After seeding your trays or containers, you must protect them from light in order to allow them to properly germinate. This period of time that you keep them covered is known as a "black out period" and usually lasts between 2-5 days. While in nature or your garden your seeds are covered with soil, for microgreens your best option is using a light and waterproof material that completely covers your soil or container. A plastic cut out or another tray works well for this. While some sources claim to use soil for topping your seeds this can lead to dirty microgreens and increased probability of fungal growth or disease. The density of the seeds planted often means the young seedlings push the soil up onto each other and away from their bases where it supports their growth. Finally, be sure to top your lid with a weight to further push the seeds into the soil. A watering can, or spray bottle can work well for this.

5. Gently Water

Gently mist or water your containers making sure not to disturb the soil and the seeds beneath it. You will have to water anywhere between every 1-3 days depending on your climate. Since small containers hold less water be ready to water these more often than larger containers. Like any container make sure not to oversaturate the water and empty the drainage plate below it after watering.

6. Wait and Harvest

For most microgreens you will be able to harvest anywhere between 10-25 days after planting. If you notice your microgreens are leaning toward one direction flip the container for more even growth. For harvesting just snip the stems near the base with a pair of scissors and use your microgreens fresh!

10 Easy Microgreens to Grow at Home

Seed quantity is based for 10"x20" propagation tray.

---

1. Amaranth

Preferred Growing Medium: *Hydroponic*
Pre-soak: *No*
Seed Rate per 1020 Tray: *1 oz*
Water Requirement: *Once every 1-2 days*
Blackout Time: *5-6 days*
Days to Germination: *2-3 days*
Days to Harvest: *10-12 days*

Amaranth is highly regarded as a mineral and vitamin rich superfood. The microgreens taste like lettuce and are even more nutritional than the mature plant. Red amaranth, which is often cultivated ornamentally, is a shiny red color that makes a beautiful garnish.

How to Use
-Add to any smoothie for a nutritious boost. Its flavor is relatively mild, but it will add an incredible mineral and vitamin content to any smoothie.
-Take your avocado toast to the next level with a bit of lime and amaranth microgreens.
-Make your breakfast extra nutritious by using them in an omelette.

---

2. Kale

Preferred Growing Medium: *Hydroponic*
Pre-soak: *No*
Seed Rate per 1020 Tray: *1 oz*
Water Requirement: *once every 1-2 days*
Blackout Time: *3-5 days*
Days to Germination: *2-3 days*
Days to Harvest: *10-12 days*

Kale is an excellent option for microgreens. Like its full size, counterpart, it's extremely nutritious and versatile. Kale seed is also readily available in most garden centers and produced by the thousands if you let your plants go to seed. Kale microgreens are milder in flavor and easier to digest than full sized Kale.

How to Use
-Mix it into your potato salad for added texture and a more nutritious profile.
-Add it to any salad for extra nutrients and a guaranteed crunch.
-Goes great in any veggie stir fry or egg scramble!

3. Radish

Preferred Growing Medium: *Hydroponic*
Pre-soak: *No*
Seed Rate per 1020 Tray: *1.2 oz*
Water Requirement: *Once a day*
Blackout time: *3-4 days*
Days to Germination: *2-3 days*
Days to Harvest: *10-12 days*

If you're looking to add a spicy kick to any meal, then radish microgreens are the way to go. These young seedlings are tender unlike the rough foliage of mature radish leaves but with a similar mustard spice to the root. These are some of the fastest seeds to germinate and prepare for harvest. They are available in both red and green leafed varieties.

How to Use
-Spice up a cheesy quesadilla or grilled cheese with a handful of these microgreens.
-Roll them up into sushi rolls for a simulated wasabi kick.
-Goes great in a creamy chicken or tuna salad!

4. Arugula

Preferred growing medium: *Hydroponic*
Pre-soak: *No*
Seed Rate per 1020 Tray: *1.2 oz*
Water requirement: *Every 1-2 days*
Blackout time: *4-6 days*
Days to germination: *2-3 days*
Days to harvest: *8-12 days*

If you're a fan of arugula, just wait until you try it as a microgreen. It's earthy like mature arugula but fresher, crisper, and a bit milder making it appealing to a wider range of audiences. It's quick to germinate and the seeds are produced in extremely large quantities if you let a plant go to seed.

How to Use
-You can use arugula microgreens just like you would regular arugula in a salad.
-Add it into any cold sandwich for a delicious arugula flavor with a crispy microgreen texture.

5. Basil

Preferred growing medium: *Hydroponic*
Pre-soak: *No*
Seed Rate per 1020 Tray: *1 oz*
Water Requirement: *Once every 1-2 days*
Blackout Time: *5-7 days*
Days to Germination: *3-4 days*
Days to Harvest: *10-14 days*

Basil microgreens are an excellent way to enjoy the fresh taste of basil without having to grow a full-size plant. These microgreens have the same aromatic flavor and properties as regular basil but in the small size of microgreens. There are many different types of basil to choose from, ranging from your Italian culinary basil or your Thai sweet basil. There is also a variety of tulsi basil which is used more as a medicinal tea.

How to Use
-Goes great with pasta or almost any Italian dish. Incorporate it directly into your tomato sauce or place on top of pizza or spaghetti.
-Place your basil microgreens directly into a broth soup like a Vietnamese Pho. Thai basil is an excellent option for this.
-Fresh bread, tomato, cheese, and basil microgreens. Need I say more?
-Place directly on top of a pesto dip as a garnish and for an extra basil kick!

6. Fenugreek

Preferred Growing Medium: *Hydroponic*
Pre-soak: *No*
Seed Rate per 1020 Tray: *1 oz*
Water Requirement: *Once every 1-2 days*
Blackout Time: *5-6 days*
Days to Germination: *3-5 days*
Days to Harvest: *18-20 days*

Fenugreek is a delicious microgreen that is extremely versatile. With a texture like bean sprout but has a slightly bitter and aromatic flavor. It is easy and quick to grow and recommended if you enjoy consuming regular fenugreek! It is also extremely high in antioxidants.

How to Use
-Add it to a bacon, lettuce, tomato sandwich for a delicious kick and texture.
-Goes great on cream of tomato or spinach soup!

7. Mizuna

Preferred Growing Medium: *Hydroponic*
Pre-soak: *No*
Seed Rate per 1020 Tray: *1 oz*
Water Requirement: *Once every 1-2 days*
Blackout time: 2-4 days
Days to Germination: *1-2 days*
Days to Harvest: *10-12 days*

Mizuna is a delicious Japanese version of arugula that is highly desired and valued as a microgreen. It goes great in both cooked and cold dishes, giving it an extra spicy and arugula like flavor!

How to Use
-Substitute it for arugula microgreens!
-Serve it on top of lentils or beans as a gorgeous and nutritious garnish.
-Mix it with cut tomato, lime, and salt for a delicious salsa or topping for bread!

8. Cilantro

Preferred Growing Medium: *Soil*

Pre-soak: *No*

Seed Rate per 1020 Tray: *2 oz*

Water Requirement: *Once every 1-2 days*

Blackout Time: *7 days*

Days to Germination: *7-14 days*

Days to Harvest: *18-20 days*

Cilantro adds a fresh and cooling taste to almost any meal and the microgreens are no different. Cilantro microgreens go great in a variety of Latin and Asian dishes, and like its mature counterpart always goes good with lime. You can use it almost identically to regular cilantro.

How to Use

-Mix with chopped onion, tomato, lime and salt for an amazing pico-de-gallo. Add avocado to the mix to make it guacamole!

-Top off any taco with cilantro microgreens as a delicious and beautiful garnish.

-Add it to Mexican rice or mix it in at the end of cooking any Mexican inspired meat dish.

9. Beet

Preferred Growing Medium: *Hydroponic*
Pre-soak: *12-24 hours in cold water*
Seed Rate per 1020 Tray: *1.2 oz*
Water requirement: *Once every 1-2 days*
Blackout Time: *6-8 days*
Days to Germination: *3-4 days*
Days to Harvest: *10-12 days*

Beet microgreens are some of the most popular because of how quickly they grow, their beautiful color, and how delicious and sweet they are. They taste very similar to the beetroot itself but sweeter and with less of the earthy beet flavor. The color is absolutely spectacular and make it a particularly beautiful garnish that is a crowd pleaser. Since chard is very closely related you can use it almost interchangeably with beet microgreens.

How to Use
-Garnish any dip, salad, or main dish with these microgreens to provide an absolutely stunning appearance.
-These go great inside sandwiches where they can provide a beet like flavor with a more pleasant texture then the beetroot itself.
-Add enough of these in a smoothie to give it a burst of red color and nutrients!

10. Mustard

Preferred Growing Medium: *Hydroponic*
Pre-soak: *No*
Seed rate per 1020 Tray: *1 oz*
Water Requirement: *Once every 1-2 days*
Blackout Time: *2-4 days*
Days to Germination: *1-2 days*
Days to Harvest: *12-14 days*

Mustard microgreens are often potent and spicy like a good horseradish or Dijon mustard. They are quick to germinate and come in many distinct varieties. The "red frill" variety provides a beautiful appearance as a garnish.

How to Use

-Mix it in directly to a stir-fry for that added mustard kick!

-Goes great with cubed potatoes or a potato salad to spice up the flavor.

-Turn a boring salad into an exciting one by throwing in a handful of mustard microgreens!

Chapter 10: Plant Propagation

One of the most wondrous and rewarding parts of gardening is building relationships with plants and having the ability to regenerate them through various means of propagation. Plants are intrinsically regenerative as they can be reproduced, often from just a single individual into potentially hundreds or thousands of individuals. Having the knowledge on how to do this can be extremely beneficial as it not only allows you to reproduce plants for your own use but also for sharing and preserving specific varieties that you enjoy cultivating and consuming.

There are several ways to propagate plants, the most common are by seed or through vegetative cutting. While you're already familiar with starting plants from seeds, vegetative cuttings are another easy way to propagate many different plant species faster and easier than it is with seeds. A vegetative cutting is essentially a stem of a plant that has been removed (usually by cutting with a knife or scissors) from a living plant and placed in the right conditions to where it grows roots and becomes a separate self-sustaining individual.

Why Propagate Your Own Plants?
While it's easy to run to a nursery and pick up a six pack of most things you'll want to cultivate in your garden, there are a wide range of reasons as to why you might choose to propagate your own plants.

-Save Money
This is the biggest no brainer for most gardeners. Why spend money purchasing plants from a nursery when you already have material you can use for growing many new plants at almost no cost.

-Acquire New Plants Easily
This is often the biggest seller for many gardeners. Knowing how to properly propagate plants allows you to reproduce plants that you may find in another garden and grow it yourself. Whether you're in a

friend's garden or a public garden it's easy to ask, "Can I take a clipping of this plant?" to which the answer is most often "Yes, of course!" This allows you to easily acquire a large diversity of plants from other gardens for absolutely no cost.

-Grow Big

If you want to grow a large quantity of a certain plant, then propagating is often the best way to do it. With time, patience, and the proper care you can make hundreds of plants from a single individual.

-Preserve Unique Genetic Materials

The diversity of cultivated plants is enormous, and nobody can grow every variety. Often you may find yourself with a unique plant that you have never seen anywhere else and can't be found in nurseries or garden stores. Knowing how to properly propagate this plant will allow you to preserve its genetics and even share or exchange them with other gardeners.

Types of Propagation

Propagation by Seed

You're probably familiar with growing plants from seed, but there are some details you should know when it comes to saving your own seed. First you should understand that not all plants are "true to seed." When a plant is "true to seed" it means that the seeds produced by that plant will grow into plants almost identical to their mother plant. For example, certain varieties of tomatoes are specialty hybrids and will produce seeds that grow into different varieties of tomato than itself. If your plant is a "hybrid" then it is likely not going to be true to seed. Another disadvantage of seeds is that some plants will take a long time to start from seeds, certain seeds even take up to a year just to germinate! Typically, smaller seeds will take longer to grow whereas larger seeds will grow more quickly.

If you ever do plan to save your seed, there are certain procedures that are recommended. Certain plants like tomatoes and melons will actually have

---

higher germination rates when fermented in their own fruit juice for several days to weeks. When preserving your seed, you will want to wash it thoroughly with water and completely dry it in the shade before storing it in an airtight container. Soaking it in hydrogen peroxide is often recommended to further sanitize it and kill any potential pathogens that may still be harbored on the seed. If your seed is not properly washed or dried, then it may end up growing mold during storage.

Propagation by Cutting

Like previously mentioned, propagation by cutting can be an easy way to reproduce a large quantity of plants in a short period of time. The benefits of this form of propagation when compared to seed, is that it is often much quicker and easier for a large variety of plants. With that said it's also important to note that some plants are easier to start from cutting while others cannot be started by cutting at all. Plants in the mint family for example are very easily propagated, often just by leaving a well-prepared clipping in water and letting it root. They can easily be identified by square stems and leaves/stems that grow in opposite directions from the same point in the stems.

Tomatoes and chilis can also be started by cutting but are often much more delicate and may require rooting hormone and more attention to properly start rooting. Other plants like lettuce, kale, or sunflowers can't be started by cutting and must be started by seed. While some plants are best to root in just plain water others are best to root directly in soil. One great benefit of cutting is that you know your new plants will be the exact same as your mother plant and it is often much faster than seed. We will go into this propagation method in more detail later.

Propagation by Ground/Air Layering

These forms of propagation are done by stimulating your plant to produce roots from a stem without removing it from the original plant. The simplest way to do this is through Ground Layering where you pull a branch or stem down and bury it into moist soil so it will grow roots. Once the roots are developed you can now disconnect it from its mother plant and move it to a new location. This is often a good propagation method for vining plants like raspberries, blackberries, or sweet potatoes. You can even place a container full of soil next to the plant you wish to propagate and bury its stem directly into the container for easy transport.

Air layering is a bit more complicated and is typically done for the propagation of fruit trees. You do this by removing the bark and inner bark of a branch and then wrapping it in moist peat moss or coco coir and plastic wrap. This stimulates the tree to produce roots into the moist material. After several months you can remove the entire branch and plant it into the ground or container of your choice.

Propagation by Tissue Culture

This will not be discussed in great detail because it is a highly advanced technique used for industrial production. This propagation technique is done by culturing specific plant cells in petri-dishes that can eventually be turned into entire mature plants. This is what is done for large scale propagation of many fruit trees, vineyard grapes, and other perennial plants you may find in a nursery.

General Principles of Propagating by Cutting

-Use the Right Tools

Always use sharp pruning shears or knives when taking a clipping. Avoid tearing or damaging the tissue at all costs. Ideally you will want to use clean tools and sanitize them with isopropyl alcohol to reduce any potential disease. Damaged tissue and unsanitary conditions can lead to bacterial and fungal infections in the cutting.

-Growth from Nodes

Nodes are special growth points found on the stems of plants where you most typically see the growth of new leaves and stems. From these nodes you can also stimulate the growth of roots which is crucial for the proper growth of cuttings. In most cases you will want stems with at least four nodes for good success. Two nodes for root growth and two nodes for foliar growth.

-Cleanliness

Being clean is important for maximizing the success of your cuttings. If placing your cuttings in water, make sure that the container is absolutely clean and that the water is pure. Avoid any soil or any foreign organic materials inside of your water. Changing the water once every other day will ensure better results but may not be necessary for hardier cuttings.

-Don't Overcrowd

One of the most common mistakes that are made when people start rooting their cuttings in water is that they place too many cuttings in the same container. Don't place more than 3-4 cuttings together and don't place different types of cuttings together in the same container. Doing both will drastically reduce your rooting success.

-Remove Excess Foliage and Keep in the Shade

Since your cuttings won't have any roots developed at first its best to remove most of the foliage from your plants. It's usually best to just leave the top two leaves of the cutting as to reduce its stress. Keep the cuttings out of direct sunlight for this same reason. In extremely dry conditions you can also make a small greenhouse from a plastic bag or clear plastic container to increase the humidity.

-Rooting Hormone

Some plants require rooting hormone in order to start producing roots. These are often applied at just a couple drops per liter of water. Do not over apply rooting hormone to your liquid as this will trigger the defense mechanism of your plants and cause it to become stressed.

-Use Fresh Growth

In most cases you will want to use the newly grown parts of the plant for cutting materials as opposed to woody old growth. This is a general rule of thumb but is not true for all plants.

-Rooting Medium

If rooting in soil, use regular potting mix with an added 20% vermiculite to the mix. You will want your soil to be moist but never too wet or you will risk rotting the cutting.

10 Easy Plants to Grow from Cutting

1. Mint	
	*All varieties of Mint are extremely easy to start by cutting. Spearmint, peppermint, apple, mint, and every herbaceous mint can be propagated easily in water. Use fresh growth, put 3-4 cuttings per container max, and don't mix different varieties in the same rooting vessel.*

-Cut a 4-8" stem of fresh growth from a mint plant of your choice making sure you have at least 4 nodes.
-Place in a clean container full of water with at least 2 nodes below water and 2 above
-After 3-5 weeks your roots should be several inches long and ready to transplant.

2. Sweet Potato

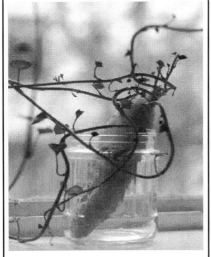

Sweet potatoes are best propagated by cutting and will actually produce more potatoes this way than other propagation methods. Sweet potato cutting should be rooted in moist soil and will root easily as long as soil does not dry out.

-Cut the ends of a sweet potato vine to have a piece at least 6" long with 4 nodes.

-Bury 3/4 of the nodes in a container full of moist soil. You can space cuttings about 6" apart in large containers.

-You can either start this process in small 1/4 gallon containers and transplant after 4-5 weeks or just use your final container if you have no issues keeping it well watered.

3. Basil

Basil can be an aggressive grower and a great one to propagate to keep in your collection year after year. There are many different types of basils and all can be propagated in the same way. Take your cuttings before the plant starts to flower for best results.

-Cut 4-8" of fresh growth avoiding any material that appears diseased. Make sure you have at least 4 nodes on your cutting.

-Remove all but the top 2 leaves of the plant.

-Place at least 2 nodes below water and 2 above.

-Transplant into water after 3-4 weeks when roots are several inches in length.

4. Sage

Sage can be easily grown as a cutting and is much easier than cultivating by seed. It is most recommended to root in soil, but you can have success rooting directly in water.

-Cut a 4-5" stem from a developed sage plant. Use newer tender growth for best results.

-Remove all but the youngest newest leaves and place 2-3 nodes into rooting soil.

-Place in the shade and water routinely but avoid oversaturating soil.

-if living in an extremely dry climate cover with a plastic bag to create a small greenhouse to trap humidity.

-Since sage is a bit trickier it's recommended to try with at least 3-4 cuttings.

5. Thyme

Thyme is another herb that takes a particularly long time to start from seed but can easily be started by cutting. Since a single plant of thyme is typically pretty slow growing, reproducing it into several plants can in the long run help you yield better harvests.

-Cut a 4-5" stem of tender growth from a mature thyme plant. Avoid using any material that is too woody but instead the fresh growth that comes from these woody stems.

-Gently remove all the leaves except for those at the tip making sure not to rip or damage the outer layer of the stem.

-Place your cutting in moist vermiculite rich soil, leaving 1-2 inches exposed to the air.

-Keep well-watered. In extremely dry climates you can improvise a greenhouse from a plastic bag placed over your container.

-After 8-10 weeks your cuttings roots should be well developed, and you can transplant it into a larger container if necessary.

6. Tomatoes

While a bit trickier than other plants tomatoes can also be propagated by cutting. This is a great way to propagate tomatoes because you know that those grown from cutting will be identical to their mother plants. Many specialty varieties are hybrids that will not stay true to seed, so cultivating it by cutting is your best option!

-Cut off side shoots from plant when they are about 6-8" long.

-Remove lower leaves and place in a container with 1/2 of the stem in water.

-Place no more than 2 cuttings per container.

-Replace water routinely and wait 3-4 weeks until roots have developed before transplanting into soil.

7. Raspberry

Raspberry is an easy plant to start by cutting other than the sharp thorns on the plant! You can use this same strategy for other varieties of raspberries and blackberries.

-Find a quick growing and fresh bramble and cut a 5-6" cutting from the tip.

-Remove leaves and place in soil with half of the cutting in the air.

-Wait 4-5 weeks until roots develop and transplant into soil.

-Alternatively, this is a good one to ground layer by burying a bramble in the ground while still connected to its mother plant and waiting for it to root!

8. Eggplant

Starting your eggplants from cutting can save you a lot of time and effort. Starting eggplants from seed can take quite a while whereas starting them from cutting will save you about 3-5 weeks of growth. They are a bit more delicate than other plants but definitely worth a shot!

-Use a side shoot from an eggplant by cutting it off from the main stem when it is 5-6" long.

-Remove all but the top leaves and place it in water or directly in rooting medium for 4-5 weeks.

-Keep it in the shade and transplant once the roots are several inches long.

9. Rosemary

Rosemary is another plant that is extremely slow to start from seed, so starting from cutting is your best option if you wish to reproduce it. There are many varieties of rosemary and all are propagated in the same way.

-Use fresh soft growth for your cutting, selecting a piece at least 4" long.
-Remove all the leaves except those at the tip and place in water.
-Wait 3-4 weeks until roots are several inches long and transplant into soil.

10. Oregano

Oregano is a hardy plant that is easily propagated by cutting. Use fresh herbaceous growth as opposed to woody stems for best results.

-Take a cutting from a soft stem about 4-6' long; avoid using woody materials.

-Remove all but the top leaves and place half of the stem into soil.

-Wait about 5-6 weeks until roots are well developed before transplanting into soil.

Genetic Development Through Cuttings

Certain varieties of plants have actually been developed by the selection of specific traits in cuttings. This often happens when a genetic mutation occurs in a plant and a cutting is taken from the genetically distinct part of the plant. This will create a distinct plant variety that may not be cultivated anywhere else! There is actually a type of sage that has been domesticated by the indigenous people of Mexico through cuttings for so long that it had stopped producing seeds and is genetically distinct from anything found in the wild! So, keep an eye out for any strange or unique growth in a plant, you may be able to make your own unique variety!

Conclusion

While this book is full of detailed information and a wide range of knowledge, know that container gardening can be achieved successfully by those at any level of experience or skill set. It is not something limited to professional gardeners. No one will ever be a complete master at this art and even the most experienced individuals will continue learning year after year. Dedication and keen observation will be the most important characters to determine your success at this endeavor.

Don't become stressed when your plants are unhappy because remember, you are still learning and even the greatest gardeners experience failure. Remember to treat your journey into the world of container gardening as a fun and fulfilling passion and not as a job or task necessary for survival. After all it's not life or death, but it's ultimately for fun with many positive externalities. You will connect deeper with the planet through your newly gained relationship with plants and your food. You will lessen your environmental impact and make this world a greener place. You may inspire your friends, family, and neighbors to start gardening. You will have a fun and fulfilling way to spend your time that will make your life fuller and more productive.

Having knowledge in container gardening is also a great skill set to have as we continue entering the digital age where man is continually more and more disconnected from nature and our food sources. It's absolutely important that people around the world start delving into urban gardening because the environmental impacts and insecurities of our modern agricultural system are now too great. We are depleting and polluting large quantities of water and land at an unsustainable rate that makes our future food security uncertain. Having knowledge in container gardening will add the certainty that if it came down to it you could start cultivating your own food in almost any landscape and environment. Knowledge is power, and ultimately the powerhouse of your brain and body is nourished by the food that you eat! So, know that with this skill set you are not only playing a role in a cultural and environmental revolution, but you are also building a skill set that will empower you and give you security in a time of many unknowns!

Final Tips and Suggestions

Work Smart Not Hard

Trying to grow tomatoes in a cold northern winter will rarely yield good results. Keep in mind your seasonality, frost dates, and your hardiness zone. Planting the right plants at the right time will save you time, money, and the stress of watching your plants suffer!

Reuse and Recycle Materials

Consider avoiding plastic materials that may end up becoming garbage. Poke holes at the bottom of eggshells, egg cartons, old milk cartons, or already used disposable cups as easy alternatives to recycle materials that would otherwise become garbage. You may have something in your garbage at the moment that still has value in its life!

More Than Just Coffee

Consider putting coffee filters at the bottom of your containers to prevent the loss of dirt through draining water. Alternatively, old shirts or fabrics work as well!

Morning Watering

Feeding in the middle of a hot day not only stresses your plants but water droplets on their leaves can burn them due to the refraction of the sunlight! Water them in the morning for healthier plants and to prevent extra water loss through evaporation.

Rainwater Harvesting

If you have gutters on your roof, direct them into a barrel or trash bin to collect this valuable resource. Not only may the rainwater be beneficial for your plants than your municipal tap water, but it will save you on irrigation costs!

Learn to Compost
Composting your kitchen scraps can be an amazing way to acquire a nutrient rich fertilizer with almost no cost or effort. There are many options for doing this, even in small apartments. You can even start a worm farm in five-gallon buckets!

Eat it All
Did you know carrot greens were edible? What about beet leaves? Sweet potato and sweet pea shoots? Even squash and pumpkin flowers! You may have more food production than you think! Investigate your plants well and understand their traditional uses or you may be letting an entire harvest go to waste!

Painted Pots
Did you know black containers absorb more heat than light colored ones? This is ideal for the winter and can provide your plants with additional warmth when the temperatures are low, but a light-colored container may be more ideal for hot summer months when it's reflecting more heat. Consider this according to the plants needs and the season when choosing the container and color. Painting containers can be a fun project but do so with waterproof paint!

Happy Gardening! ☺

Resources

Allman, M. (2016, October 07). Daylight Hours to Grow Lettuce. Retrieved September 09, 2020, from https://homeguides.sfgate.com/daylight-hours-grow-lettuce-70987.html

Arbuckle, K. (2016, October 07). How to Grow & Feed Eggplants. Retrieved September 09, 2020, from https://homeguides.sfgate.com/grow-feed-eggplants-44304.html

Container Gardens. (n.d.). Retrieved September 09, 2020, from https://www.bhg.com/gardening/container/

Degnan, S. (2016, October 07). How to Care for a Thyme Plant. Retrieved September 09, 2020, from https://homeguides.sfgate.com/care-thyme-plant-24088.html

Donaldson, S., McHoy, P., & Donaldson, S. (2011). *Container gardening: The complete practical guide to container gardening, indoors and outdoors.* New York: Metro Books.

Elzer-Peters, K. (2012). *Beginner's illustrated guide to gardening: Techniques to help you get started.* Brentwood, TN: Cool Springs Press.

Engel, H. (2016, October 07). Tips on Growing Raspberry Bushes. Retrieved September 09, 2020, from https://homeguides.sfgate.com/tips-growing-raspberry-bushes-25644.html

Franks, E., &Richardson, J. (2009). *Microgreens: A guide to growing nutrient-packed greens.* Layton, UT: Gibbs Smith.

Gardening in pots: How to grow healthy pot plants. (1988). Alexandria, N.S.W.: Federal Pub.

Geiger, P. (2012). *Farmers' almanac: Calculated for the United States for the year of our Lord 2013.* Lewiston, Me.: Farmers' Almanac.

How to grow all kinds of plants. McGregor's guide to gardening. (1932). Springfield, OH: McGregorBros.

Lestrieux, E. D., & Evans, H. (1990). *The art of gardening in pots.* Woodbridge, Suffolk, England: Antiques Collectors' Club.

MacCaskey, M., & Elmore, A. L. (2003). *Lowe's creative ideas for outdoor living.* Menlo Park, CA: Sunset Pub.

Old Farmer's Almanac. (n.d.). Broccoli. Retrieved September 09, 2020, from https://www.almanac.com/plant/broccoli

Pennington, A. (2019, May 01). The Easiest Vegetable You Can Grow Indoors. Retrieved September 09, 2020, from https://www.thekitchn.com/what-you-need-to-know-about-growing-arugula-indoors-244755

PLANTS AND SEEDS. (n.d.). Retrieved September 09, 2020, from https://parkseed.com/plants/c/plants/

Raworth, J., & Bradley, V. (1998). *The complete guide to indoor gardening.* New York: Abbeville Press.

Simpson, M. (2017, November 21). Simple Way to Grow Strawberries. Retrieved September 09, 2020, from https://homeguides.sfgate.com/simple-way-grow-strawberries-41523.html

Donaldson, S., McHoy, P., & Donaldson, S. (2011). *Container gardening: The complete practical guide to container gardening, indoors and outdoors*. New York: Metro Books.

Franks, E., &Richardson, J. (2009). *Microgreens: A guide to growing nutrient-packed greens*. Layton, UT: Gibbs Smith.

Hey there!

We hope you enjoyed reading Easy Peasy Crops in Pots.

Comments and suggestions are welcome! Feel free to leave a review over at Amazon or send them to:

thesufficienceallegiant@gmail.com

Printed in Great Britain
by Amazon

55503615R00080